# COCAINE AN

*Also by Philip Bean*

BARBARA WOOTTON: Selected Writings
  (*editor with Vera G. Seal*)
Volume 1: CRIME AND THE PENAL SYSTEM I
Volume 2: CRIME AND THE PENAL SYSTEM II
Volume 3: SOCIAL AND POLITICAL THOUGHT
Volume 4: ECONOMIC AND METHODOLOGICAL THOUGHT

POLICING AND PRESCRIBING (*editor with D. K. Whynes*)

# Cocaine and Crack

## Supply and Use

Edited by

## Philip Bean
*Reader in Criminology and*
*Director, the Midlands Centre for Criminology and Criminal Justice,*
*University of Loughborough*

## St. Martin's Press

First published in Great Britain 1993 by
THE MACMILLAN PRESS LTD
Houndmills, Basingstoke, Hampshire RG21 2XS
and London
Companies and representatives
throughout the world

A catalogue record for this book is available from the British Library.

ISBN 0–333–55831–6 hardcover
ISBN 0–333–58681–6 paperback

Printed in Hong Kong

---

First published in the United States of America 1993 by
Scholarly and Reference Division,
ST. MARTIN'S PRESS, INC.,
175 Fifth Avenue,
New York, N.Y. 10010

ISBN 0–312–08939–2

Library of Congress Cataloging-in-Publication Data
Cocaine and crack: supply and use / edited by Philip Bean.
p.   cm.
Includes index.
ISBN 0–312–08939–2
1. Cocaine habit—Great Britain.   2. Crack (Drug)—Great Britain.
3. Drug abuse—Great Britain.   I. Bean, Philip.
HV5840.G7C6   1993
362.29'8'0941—dc20                                    92–25573
                                                          CIP

# Contents

# Notes on the Contributors

**Philip Bean** is Reader in Criminology and Director of the Midlands Centre of Criminology and Criminal Justice at the University of Loughborough. Prior to that he was Senior Lecturer in the Department of Social Policy, University of Nottingham. He has published widely in the field of drug abuse, recently conducting research in crack/cocaine, and ecstasy. His publications go back to 1974 and extend from *The Social Context of Drugs* (1974) to *Policing and Prescribing* (1992).

**Jason Ditton** is Senior Lecturer and Director of the Criminology Research Unit at the University of Glasgow. His previous publications include *Part-time Crime*; *Controlology* and *The View from Goffman*. He is currently completing a book on cocaine use in Scotland, and is beginning to research patterns of ecstasy use.

**Michael Farrell** is a research psychiatrist at the National Addiction Centre at the Institute of Psychiatry. His interests include research in training in the prevention and treatment of substance problems. He has a particular interest in problems in young people and HIV and drug problems; and in the social policy aspects of substance misuse prevention.

**Jane Goodsir** has worked on legal issues concerning drug users since the late 1970s. She became interested in drugs cases because of the civil liberties issues they raised. She was Director of Release, the national drugs charity for six years until 1991. At Release, she campaigned against injustice affecting individual drug users, as well as running a more conventional legal and drugs advice service. Educated at University College London, and the University of Bristol, she has written on a range of drug-related legal and management issues. She is currently conducting research on the management and professional issues affecting organisations helping drug users.

**Heidi Safia Mirza** is Senior Lecturer in Social Science, South Bank University. She has taught Afro-American Studies at Brown University, USA, and Sociology at the University of London. She has worked as a researcher on the Day-Care Project at the Thomas

Coram Research Unit, Institute of Education, and The Drug Information Project, Goldsmiths' College, University of London. She is the author of *Young, Female and Black* (1992).

**Joy Mott** is a Principal Research Officer at the Home Office Research and Planning Unit. She is responsible for planning and managing research on drug misuse with a particular interest in drugs misuse and crime.

**Geoffrey Pearson** is Wates Professor of Social Work in the University of London, Goldsmiths' College. He is Associate Editor of the *British Journal of Criminology* and a member of the British Society of Criminology's national council. His published work includes *The Deviant Imagination* (1975); *Hooligan: A History of Respectable Fears* (1983); *Young People and Heroin* (1985); and *The New Heroin Users* (1987).

**Stewart Phillips** worked as a researcher on the Drug Information Project, Goldsmiths' College, University of London. He has worked for the Inner London Probation Service, and is currently a postgraduate at the London School of Economics.

**Harry Shapiro** has been employed at the Institute for the Study of Drug Dependence in London since 1979 both as an Information Officer and currently as Head of Publications. He is also the author of several ISDD publications and deputy editor of the ISDD journal *Druglink*.

**H. B. Spear** joined the Home Office Drugs Inspectorate in 1952, after completing National Service in the RAF, and retired as Chief Inspector in 1986. In that time he witnessed most of the important changes in the British drug misuse problem, which he is now attempting to write up, while also pursuing his ancestors through the parish records of Devon and Cornwall.

**John Strang** is Consultant Psychiatrist in Drug Dependence, Drug Unit, National Addiction Centre, Maudsley Hospital, London and was previously involved in the development of drug services in the North West of England during the early/mid 1980s. He is now actively involved in the development of clinical services for drug misusers which also constitute a base for clinical research studies, while also involved in the provision of training through a new Drug Training Unit at the Maudsley. He is a member of the Advisory Council on the Misuse of Drugs, and also a member of the Expert Advisory Group on AIDS at the Department of Health. He is the Consultant Adviser on Drug Services to the Department of Health. He has written extensively in the scientific and popular press about drug misuse and co-edited a book on AIDS and drug misuse.

**Sujata Unnithan** qualified from Liverpool University Medical School in 1985 and is currently Senior Registrar at the Drug Dependency Unit, Maudsley Hospital, London. She has conducted research into the psychiatric phenomena associated with cocaine use and other papers relating to relapse and emergency presentation of drug misusers. Her current interests include research into pain and opiate dependency and the behavioural pharmacological aspects of drug misuse.

# Cocaine and Crack: An Introduction

Philip Bean

In the late 1980s dire predictions were made of a new drug crisis in Britain. The drug was cocaine, with 'crack' its potent derivative. *The Sunday Times* (7 January 1990) warned that Britain faced a cocaine epidemic, as Columbian drug barons found it increasingly difficult to smuggle drugs into the saturated United States market, and pointed out that Britain had become the final destination for huge consignments of Columbian cocaine which were shipped direct from South America into Europe or through the United States. *The Sunday Times* added somewhat pointedly that customs seizures for cocaine reached 420 kg or 935 lb in 1989, up 50 per cent on 1988. And, for good measure, it added that crack was ten times more addictive than cocaine.

This report rather typifies the media response to the modern cocaine crisis of the late 1980s. The listed amount of cocaine seized was, of course, correct, and easily verified from the figures taken from HM Customs and Excise returns. Yet what it did not say was that most of the 420 kg seized in 1989 were of one consignment in transit to Amsterdam. Moreover, statements such as 'crack is 10 times more addictive than cocaine' or 'Britain has become the final destination for huge consignments of Columbian cocaine' were either simply wrong, or based on assumptions which were highly questionable.

*The Sunday Times* was not the only newspaper to predict an epidemic or threaten the cocaine Armageddon. Others fell into the same trap (see Chapter 3). Yet eight months later, on 10 August 1990, *The Times* noted in an editorial that 'no evidence of the threatened crack explosion has yet been found'. *The Times* also traced some of the assumptions behind the earlier fears and found them questionable. The main one was the belief that the trend in the American black city ghettoes would sooner or later produce itself in Britain, especially in cities with a significant Afro-Caribbean population. Yet *The Times* noted that West Indians in Britain had little in common with blacks in the USA except their skin colour. Their history and culture are different, so is their pattern of concentration

1

and their degree of participation in the national economy. It concluded, 'The British welfare state offers a more sophisticated system
of support to disadvantaged communities than does the American
one' (10 August 1990). This more sober assessment takes account of
factors other than the economic intentions of the Columbian drug
barons and the rather simpleminded view that the USA inevitably
exports its drug problems.

Much of the press coverage in Britain in 1989 or 1990 created the
impression that crack, and the drug from which it is derived, cocaine,
were new to Britain. Yet cocaine, as Bing Spear and Joy Mott show
(Chapter 2) is a well-established drug among British users. It also has
a long history of control. In the circumstances, one wonders why it
attracted so little interest generally, apart from the late 1980s. It was
traditionally a drug favoured by the middle classes, possibly making it
something of a minority drug, but not exclusively, as there were
cocaine epidemics in Britain as far back as the First World War.
Indeed, until 1961, cocaine was the only drug to promote its own
piece of legislation, the 1923 Dangerous Drugs Amendment Act.
This was introduced as a result of domestic changes in consumption,
i.e. as opposed to changes at the international level (Bean, 1974,
p. 32). Cocaine was also used regularly in the 1960s, mixed with
heroin by the street junkies of that era; it was supplied legally with
other drugs, some of which were passed illegally to other users. There
were, for example, 86 prosecutions for illegal possession in 1967
rising to 162 in 1970 (Bean, 1974, p. 108). What was new in the late
1980s was crack – yet crack is only a different form of cocaine, or
rather the same form but with a different delivery system.

Cocaine, like the opiates, is a well-established and well-known
drug of abuse. It comes from the leaf of the coca plant (*Erthroxylon
coca*) which has been used for social and medicinal purposes for at
least 5000 years (ibid., 1974). The coca leaves were chewed by South
American Indians, who recognised their stimulant properties. In the
modern era cocaine has been used, or rather abused in one of three
ways; first, by snorting, which means inhaling the drug through the
nose; second, by intravenous injection – usually mixed with a de-
pressant such as heroin, the combination of which produces a greater
sense of euphoria; and thirdly, by smoking – the latter the most
effective and fastest way of delivering concentrated doses to the
brain. For abusers, the speed of onset and the reported intensity of
the experience are important determinants of its use.

Cocaine has certain medical properties, though its medical use is

1 Plan /1 3 · 95

decreasing. It is a topical anaesthetic: that is, it has the rather curious property of being an anaesthetic when applied to the top of the skin but a stimulant when snorted, injected or smoked. It was once a popular anaesthetic in dentistry, though its use in that form was discontinued by the 1920s (see Chapter 2). It is still manufactured in the UK for legitimate medical use (including when it is provided under prescription to users) by May and Baker. Its medical use nowadays is largely confined to ear, nose and throat prescriptions and eye-drops. Cocaine hydrochloride based elixirs are still prepared for the alleviation of distress associated with terminal conditions. They are sometimes combined with an equal amount of diamorphine (heroin), usually 5 mg each – and sometimes chlorpromaxine. These solutions are unstable and deteriorate on standing. Cocaine free base is not available for use in medicine.

When we talk of cocaine, we usually mean cocaine hydrochloride, which is a fine, white, crystalline powder. Cocaine hydrochloride is made from the treatment of coca paste, sometimes called 'basuco', a cheap, low-quality product derived from the coca leaf (see Inciardi, 1988). Cocaine hydrochloride is the salt form of the drug – hydrochloric acid having been used to produce the salt. The base form, usually called crack, is produced by adding sodium bicarbonate (baking powder), ammonia or caustic soda. Cocaine hydrochloride, like all salts, is unsuitable for smoking since it vaporises at very high temperatures which then destroys the drug. The base form melts more easily and vaporises at lower temperatures (at 98°C compared with 195°C for the salt), hence the need to change to the base. This makes it ideal for smoking. There is nothing new about crack: it is simply the converted base form of a salt created by using an alkali. The active part of the drug remains unchanged whichever form is used, and the effects in the human body are the same whether the base or salt form is ingested – though it is thought the response may be more intense with the base than with the salt. To say therefore that 'crack' is a new drug is misleading: crack is cocaine. All the properties and the impurities in cocaine will therefore remain in crack; the only difference between crack and cocaine is the delivering system.

The base form is quick and simple to make – that is, the base form is readily converted from the salt – though it is, of course, also possible to make it from the paste form. The manufacture of crack does not require sophisticated facilities, and the chemicals required to convert the salt to its base can be legally obtained. Crack manufacture is a cottage industry requiring no hazardous apparatus, unlike that in the production of cocaine freebase which involves a volatile solvent such as ether. Crack is often referred to as 'freebase', and the method of conversion is called 'freebasing'. Freebase is a more sophisticated technique producing a different form of the base – as one would expect when ether is used. However, throughout this volume, some authors have wanted to use the term 'freebase' and I have not wanted to insist on uniformity of terminology. There is no real uniformity of terms anyway; most terms are used without precision and I have not wanted to impose certainty where there is little. For my part, though others may use the term differently, crack is not released cocaine in its base form but simply the basic form of the salt. It requires little more than water, sodium bicarbonate and a microwave oven, though household ammonia can be substituted for sodium bicarbonate. This is the drug that appears on the streets rather than the more sophisticated ether product where the base is set free. In its popular form, i.e. the cottage industry variant, crack appears as a hard, creamy-white set of crystals, with fewer impurities than the salt. It can be marketed and sold as 'rocks'. (Sometimes crack is a dark brown colour, depending on the method used and the amount of impurities in the cocaine hydrochloride.) These rocks were sold at between £25 and £40 each in 1991; they weigh about 100 mg.

The stimulant properties of cocaine have long been known, providing it with a favoured place among certain literary figures. Freud, for example, believed in its value for the treatment of morphine addicts and in 1884 advocated its use as an euphorant. Ernest Jones, his biographer, says that Freud was in danger of becoming a public menace but, after increasing his friend Fleischl's miseries by trying to cure his morphine addiction with cocaine, and after having a patient die after repeated use, Freud too recognised and accepted its dangers (see Bean, 1974, p. 33). Cocaine itself, although a stimulant, has shortlived effects which users describe as producing feelings of well-being, exhilaration, great physical strength and increased mental capacity. Cocaine also suppresses appetite and causes insomnia. Once the effects have worn off, users may feel depressed and tired. The psychological effects of smoking crack are simply an exaggeration of those from taking cocaine. The effects, however, wear off quite rapidly in about 12 minutes to be followed by depression and anxiety (Siegal, 1982). Harry Shapiro reports that with large doses and/or periods of continued use effects may include hallucinations while depression and anxiety may develop leading to suicidal feelings and paranoia. The dysphoria is alleviated by smoking more crack or by taking drugs such as heroin or tranquillisers to take the edge off the anxiety and depression, or to induce sleep (Shapiro, 1989) (see also Glossop, 1987).

Clearly, using cocaine causes problems, some physical and some psychological. But, as we show throughout this book, some of these problems are overstated – perhaps deliberately so, to produce certain political ends. Consider the so-called 'crack babies' supposedly born addicted to cocaine who would die, it was said, if not treated; Harry Shapiro believes these claims are often exaggerated and cites medical evidence to US Congressional hearings which indicate the claims are erroneous. 'The cocaine addicted infant gets over the drug in about one or two weeks . . . If you just leave the babies in the nursery for a couple of weeks or a month, they'll do O.K.' (Shapiro, 1989, p. 142). But at the same time I do not wish to go too far in the other direction and say there are no dangers. There are, and some are serious. In some cases cocaine use causes death, by respiratory failure. Users talk of perspiring heavily, being deeply suspicious and overwhelmed by the experience. All of which presumably imply that treatment of some sort should be available.

John Strang, Michael Farrell and Sujata Unnithan (Chapter 7) point to the difficulties in speaking of treatment for cocaine users, for the types of treatment vary with the forms in which the drug is taken. For the practising clinician, however, it becomes well-nigh impossible to separate the effects of cocaine from the effects of other drugs and the lifestyle of the users. Many are poly-users, streetwise and street-junkies whose lives are chaotic and dominated by the activities of their fellow junkies, the police and the availability (or lack of it) of the drugs of their choice. However, as John Strang *et al.* say, the method of use is a critical factor in treatment outcomes, the speed of onset being the most important. Where there is a 'rush', especially that created by intravenous use, treatment outcomes are less favourable. Small wonder that by their mid-thirties most street-junkies give up – what Geoffrey Pearson describes as 'taking early retirement' from a lifestyle more hectic and life-threatening than almost any other occupation. To know or say that drug users in general and cocaine users in particular seek treatment provides no information about what the treatment should be. More cocaine, perhaps? Or something else? Tranquillisers, perhaps, as provided by some physicians? Or a less direct form of intervention offering a therapeutic-type treatment arrived at doing something about their lifestyles? John Strang *et al.* set out the parameters of treatments available, listing the range and options available (Chapter 7).

What is clear from John Strang's chapter is that we know little and in Britain do even less about treatment for cocaine users in spite of the drug's existence and its popularity dating back at least 100 years (cocaine hydrochloride was identified in 1860 and its effects were well-known and well-documented by the turn of the century). But this brings into play two other questions: is there a satisfactory treatment available and should one be provided, given that there is? That is, should a group of users producing self-inflicted injuries expect and have treatment available for them? The answer, as John Strang *et al.* show, depends on many considerations, as well as our knowledge of the medical condition cocaine is said to produce.

Much of the literature of the late 1980s, especially that from America, was of an evangelical persuasion. It spoke of cocaine as being 'highly addictive', or 'the most addictive substance known to man': so much so, that one American DEA agent said, 'they've had to redefine addiction when it comes to cocaine' (Stutman, 1989). Without going into these claims at the moment (see Chapter 2) we nevertheless need to cast a sceptical eye on them. Harry Shapiro gives results of another American study which seems more sober and more carefully constructed than most. 'Everyone who tries crack will not like the high and everyone who likes the high will not become instantly addicted' (Shapiro, 1989). Perhaps, in the absence of more detailed research, we should leave the matter there.

The absence of that data, especially the extent of use, has been a persistent problem of drug research in Britain, whether for cocaine or not. Chapter 1 provides information on the data currently available at the national level on the nature and extent of use: Shapiro's conclusion shows how tentative one must be, but his careful review of the situation stands out as a model of its kind. Clearly, more local studies are required. To this end, Jason Ditton (Chapter 4) is able to provide more extensive information based on his research into Scottish cocaine users, showing how they are part of a different drug culture with different aims and objectives. Jason Ditton's study is one of the few detailed research studies currently taking place in the UK. His results are therefore of immense importance. Another equally important study from Geoffrey Pearson, Haidi Satia Mirza and Stewart Phillips also provides information on the London scene, showing that stereotypes of typical users are rarely valid – especially those which suggest crack is entirely linked to the black population. As Geoffrey Pearson *et al.* show, the conclusions one arrives at depend on the population sampled. Most studies, it seems, rely on a rather restricted methodology, hence the restricted results (see Chapter 5).

The British system of drug control has always relied on the twin pillars of prescribing and policing (Whynes and Bean, 1991). There is little cocaine-prescribing in Britain in the early 1990s and even less for crack. Prescribing maintenance drugs seems to have gone out of fasion temporarily. The Home Office say that the amount of prescribing cocaine is limited to a few doctors in a few treatment centres and the extent of prescribing crack is almost wholly confined to one or two physicians in Merseyside.

The policing matters are defined by the 1971 Misuse of Drugs Act. Cocaine, its various salts and the leaves of the coca plant, are controlled under Class A of that Act. (Other class A drugs include heroin, LSD, pethadine). Coca leaf is under a set of regulations that envisage no medical uses so it will be supplied or possessed only by persons licensed by the Home Secretary for research or other special purposes. As stated above, cocaine and its salts can be prescribed and are legitimately used in medicines; otherwise it is illegal to possess, produce or supply the drug – and illegal also to allow premises to be used for producing or supplying cocaine. Bing Spear and Joy Mott report that concern among parliamentarians over the sale of cocaine kits in London led to the inclusion of a clause in the Drug Trafficking Offences Act 1986 which prohibited the sale of any article which may be used or adapted to be used (whether by itself or in combination with another article or other articles) in the administration of a controlled drug. It seems hypodermic syringes were excluded. This was not Britain's first drug paraphernalia law: under the 1920 Dangerous Drugs Act it was an offence merely to possess any equipment for the preparation of opium. This restriction is still in force and *The Lancet* sees a logical justification for including base pipes used in cocaine freebasing to be similarly included (see also *The Lancet*, 7 November 1987, p. 1062; and see Chapter 3).

The control of illegal cocaine is through the Customs and Excise and the police. Seizures of cocaine by HM Customs are, of course, indicative of their strategic success. They also act as an indicator of the amount of use within Britain generally – the more seized the greater the use. Seizures have considerable descriptive and predictive qualities – about how much exists now and how much will exist in the future.

*Table* 1.1    Cocaine seizures (in kg) 1984–89

| | |
|---|---|
| 1984 | 35 |
| 1985 | 79 |
| 1986 | 99 |
| 1987 | 360 |
| 1988 | 282 |
| 1989 (up to 1 April) | 202 |

*Source*   Home Affairs Comittee Report, 1989

The figures show a dramatic increase, especially in 1987 where the 360 kg seized included one consignment of 208 kg (or 57.7 per cent of the total). There was a slight fall in 1988 but the 1989 figures which are for four months only show an even greater increase (HMSO, 1989).

The number of seizures of cocaine was 510 in 1985, rising to 618 in 1988, with 632 people found guilty in 1985 compared with 591 in 1988, i.e. a rather unexpectedly low level set alongside the high amounts seized by Customs. One explanation for the discrepancy is that the customs seizures were not destined for the UK market anyway – and indeed, as mentioned, that large seizure in 1987 of 208 kg was thought to be *en route* to Holland and passing through Heathrow when it was seized. Of course, the more drugs found on entry the less problem throughout: theoretically, 1 kg of cocaine saves 1000 prosecutions of a one-gram lot thereafter (though it never works quite so simply).

If cocaine is presented as a dangerous and deadly drug, then protection from that drug and its effects is sought – and if that means trampling over people's rights, then so be it. What price rights where souls are to be saved and people to be protected? Jane Goodsir (Chapter 6) illustrates some of the civil rights issues involved in cocaine use or rather some civil rights issues that cocaine use has brought into focus. As Jane Goodsir says, fear of drug use has led to justifications for repressive views where rights seem to be ignored. We should never forget there are worse things than taking drugs. In the heat of the moment, when a drug scare arises, we may justify removing users' rights. If we do, the price we pay is a less tolerant society.

This book is the first in the UK to draw attention to the nature, use and supply of cocaine – which, it must be said, has only risen to prominence as a result of crack, and the threatened epidemic. Crack itself was used as far back as the 1980s but did not catch on for a decade or so. It is, as I have said, only a different form of cocaine and not a separate drug. This is a book mainly about cocaine, but consequently also about crack. In spite of the length of time in which cocaine has been used in Britain, it has not claimed much attention, though in 1989 there were 529 new notifications of cocaine users (the largest was heroin with 4883 followed by methadone with 682 and cocaine was third). If this book achieves anything it will have produced some information on cocaine and its use, and shed some light on areas which have remained hitherto darkened.

## ACKNOWLEDGEMENTS

All editors are faced with decisions about the type of book to be produced – in this case whether to go for a large numbers of authors and short chapters or the other way round. I thought it best to have few authors and longish chapters, if only because it seemed more important to cover a small number of topics rather than go for the wide sweep of the arguments. Anyway, with too little information available, it seemed necessary to inform as well as debate, and in doing so cover what seems to be the major or critical aspects; treatment, use, control, supply and the rights of users. Hopefully that is what has been achieved, I leave it to others to provide more detailed arguments.

I would like to thank all those involved in the production of this book, the authors for their enthusiasm and eagerness to produce their chapters and for the many others who helped with its production. Special thanks are due to Mrs Vivian Dhaliwal who helped with a number of matters relating to presentation of the manuscript, and for her valued secretarial assistance.

Philip Bean

REFERENCES

Bean, P. T. (1974) *The Social Control of Drugs* (London: Martin Robertson).
—— (1990) 'Use and supply of crack/cocaine in Nottingham', Report to the Home Office Research and Planning Unit.
Gossop, M. (1987) 'Beware Cocaine', *British Medical Journal*, Vol. 295, 17 October, p. 945.
HMSO (1989) *Crack: The threat of hard drugs in the next decade*, Home Affairs Committee (Interim report), House of Commons 19 July.
Inciardi, J. (1988) 'Beyond cocaine; basuco, crack and other coca products', *Contemporary Drug Problems*, Vol. 14, no. 3, pp. 461–92.
*The Lancet* (1987) 'Crack', 7 November, pp. 1061–3.
Shapiro, H. (1989) 'Crack – the story so far', *Health Education Journal*, Vol. 48, no. 3, pp. 140–4.
Siegel, R. K. (1982) 'Cocaine smoking', *Journal of Psychoactive Drugs*, Vol. 14, no. 4, pp. 318–35.
Stutman, R. M. (1989) 'Crack: its effect on a city and law enforcement response', paper given to the 9th Annual National Drugs Conference of Assistant Chief Police Officers in Wales (April) Nimco.
Whynes, D. K. and Bean, P. T., eds. (1991) *Policing and Prescribing* (London: Macmillan).

# 1 Where Does All the Snow Go? – The Prevalence and Pattern of Cocaine and Crack Use in Britain

Harry Shapiro

Cocaine or, rather, extracts of coca leaf, were widely available in the nineteenth century as an ingredient of many popular patent medicines and tonics. However, some concern over its addictive potential saw cocaine included in the 1908 Pharmacy Act. Later, via the Defence of the Realm Act, following the First World War scare that prostitutes were giving the drug to soldiers, cocaine passed into the Dangerous Drugs legislation of 1921 (Berridge and Edwards, 1987; see also Chapter 3).

During the 1920s, the drug had a sufficiently high profile in Britain's 'yellow press' for the novelist Dorothy L. Sayers to make cocaine distribution among the 'fast set', the key to her very popular novel *Murder Must Advertise*. However, until very recently, little was heard about the drug apart from occasional media stories about cocaine use mainly among film and pop stars. Even in America, concern about the use of cocaine in the general population is only a phenomenon of the 1980s (Johnson, 1987).

Cocaine's limited prevalence in Britain since the 1950s has probably been determined by at least two main factors. Firstly, the widespread availability of cheap amphetamine, either in pill form diverted from pharmaceutical sources (in the sixties) or illicitly home-produced amphetamine sulphate powder (from the mid-seventies onwards). Secondly, cocaine is an expensive commodity, currently anything up to four times the price per gram of amphetamine for a drug with a much shorter duration of action. In June 1991 the average street price across the UK for 1 gram of amphetamine sulphate was £12–15; for cocaine hydrochloride, £75–100; for crack (about four rocks), £75–100.

Recently, however, cocaine has been making the headlines; first because customs seizures of cocaine hydrochloride powder have been steadily rising and, more specifically, because of concern during 1989 about a predicted 'epidemic' of crack – a smokeable form of powdered cocaine.

Information about the prevalence and consequently the patterns of cocaine and crack use in Britain is extremely patchy and incomplete; 'Much has been written in the press about the alleged growth of cocaine consumption. There does not, however, appear to have been any substantial research on the subject at all in the UK' (Wagstaff and Maynard 1988).

So what hard information do we have? Firstly, there are the seizure statistics provided by Customs and Excise and the police. The amount of cocaine seized has been rising since as long ago as 1983, but in 1986, there was a fourfold increase from just over 100 kg to over 400 kg and (with the exception of 1988) it has risen from this baseline ever since to a level in 1991 of over 1000 kg (Fig. 1). The major source country has been Colombia, using newly-established trading routes via Spain and Portugal into Europe. Customs have also seized cocaine brought in mainly by women in single-kilo amounts from the Caribbean and Eastern seaboard of the USA.

The reason given by police and customs for the increases in cocaine seizures has been that the American market for the drug has been saturated, prompting the cocaine producers of South America to seek alternative markets. However, it seems more likely that there has been overproduction in the producer countries which has necessitated the search for wider rather than different markets (Royal Canadian Mounted Police, 1986). In 1985 the House of Commons Home Office Committee visited the United States. Commenting on their visit in the subsequent *Misuse Of Hard Drugs (Interim Report)*, they opined, 'We believe, from all that we saw and heard, that as the American market becomes saturated the flood of hard drugs will cross the Atlantic' (House of Commons, 1985). Yet despite these and other warnings from politicians, the inevitable taboid press coverage during 1985–86 and the undeniably marked rise in cocaine seizures, we have yet to experience any 'explosion' of cocaine use in the UK (see also Chapter 4). One senior policeman offered the view that better intelligence, greater international cooperation and initiatives such as the Drug Trafficking Offences Act would prove decisive in preventing the UK repeating the US experience (Hewitt, 1987). Nor has the country been deluged in a tidal wave of crack. In 1990 crack

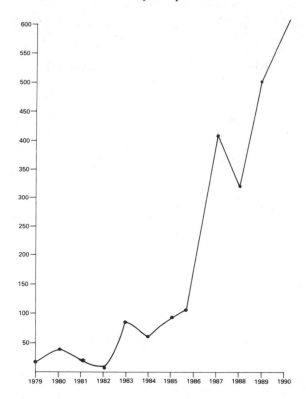

*Figure* 1.1   Cocaine seizures in England and Wales, 1984–89
Source: National Drugs Intelligence Unit, *Drug Seizure Statistics*, 1990.

seizures were running at about 15 per cent of all seizures of cocaine (Home Office Drugs Inspectorate, 1990) but, while numbers of seizures rose from 12 in 1987 to 352 in 1990, this still amounted to less than one kg of the drug (National Drugs Intelligence Unit, 1991).

Numbers of seizures of all forms of cocaine remained relatively stable until 1989 when the figure rose by 146 per cent from 829 to 2045 (Fig. 1.2). In 1990 numbers of seizures dropped by 240 although the weight seized that year rose by 22 per cent from 499 to 611 kg. The total of 1805 seizures in 1990 included over 1000 Metropolitan Police seizures, three-quarters of all police cocaine seizures (Home Office 1991) (Fig. 1.3).

Between 1988 and 1989, cannabis seizures by the Metropolitan Police rose sharply by 45 per cent. It is possible that, because of the

*Cocaine and Crack*

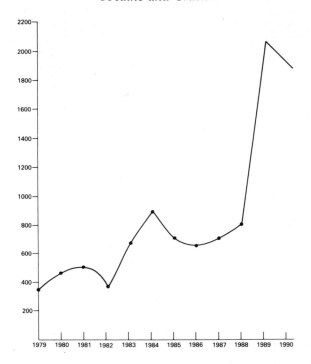

*Figure* 1.2    Numbers of cocaine seizures by Customs and police, 1979–90

Source:  National Drugs Intelligence Unit, *Drug Seizure Statistics*, 1990.
*Home Office Statistical Bulletin*, issue 19/91, September 1991.

crack scare, the Metropolitan Police have been targeting those they
believe might be potential users and, in the process of increased 'stop
and search' activity, have been finding more cannabis. Black communities in London have been increasingly convinced that the advent
of crack has given the police a new 'excuse' for harassing black people
(*Searchlight*, 1990). A recent study in Lewisham, South London,
found that 'whereas 85 per cent of crack users seen by other agencies
are white, 95 per cent of crack users arrested by the police are black.
It would seem . . . that the police have targeted black people and
black communities in their operations directed against crack and
cocaine misuse' (Mirza *et al.*, 1991). The then-director of the Community Drug Project in south London, Steve Tippell, commented
that by concentrating enforcement efforts in the denser areas of black
population, the police were fulfilling their own prophecies, 'in a sense

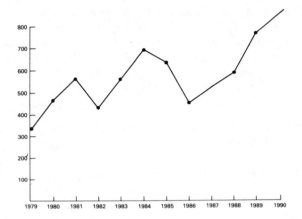

*Figure* 1.3 Persons found guilty, cautioned or dealt with for cocaine offences, 1979–90

Source: *Home Office Statistical Bulletin*, issue 19/91, September 1991.

what you look for you find – and that doesn't say much about overall patterns of drug use' (Gillman, 1990).

So what do the enforcement statistics actually tell us about the prevalence of cocaine use? The question as to whether it is supply – or demand-side enforcement measures that are the more effective in reducing consumption remains unresolved. Thus, extrapolating from drug seizure figures is always a precarious business. For example, with no national prevalence statistics available, it is impossible to say for sure what increased seizures actually mean in terms of overall consumption. If seizures go up, does this mean we are stopping more of the drug coming into the country through increased vigilance or special targeting, or does it just mean that more is getting through, bearing in mind that it is widely believed that only a relatively small percentage of drugs destined for the UK is actually seized? Alternatively, if seizures go down, does this mean that the smugglers have been frightened off by more stringent searching, or are they just more devious at hiding the drugs, or has demand fallen? One possible indicator of what is happening with supply and demand is the price on the streets. During question-time at the 1991 Customs press conference on seizures, it was revealed that the prices of drugs such as cocaine and heroin had remained relatively stable. One obvious conclusion from this is that seizures have had little impact on overall supply. If they had, one would expect the price to have risen sharply, although one might also speculate that the price might be kept artificially high by dealers to maintain the 'status' of the drug among users (particularly the relatively well-off user). However, there is no evidence of this and it could only be ascertained by fieldwork of a kind which has yet to be done. In pointing out the doubtful efficacy of targeting major drug importers, Nicholas Dorn has commented,

> The proportion of the retail ('street') price of illegal drugs that is accounted for by the importation price is very small – around 10% for cocaine in the United States. The greater part of the retail price is accounted for by the price differentials between importers and retailers. It follows that one would have to seize a quite high proportion of imports to shift the price at importation levels up sufficiently to make much difference to retail prices and hence consumption . . . The seizure rate would have to rise several hundred per cent in order to raise retail prices enough to dent demand. No known method of interdiction . . . can achieve this. (Dorn, 1989)

How does the amount seized relate to the potential numbers of users? To be able to make any comment on this, we need to start with the numbers of those notified to the Home Office by doctors as being cocaine-dependent. As with all the statistical evidence of cocaine use, the numbers of notified cocaine addicts has been rising steadily. In the ten-year period from 1979 to 1989, the number of new addicts has risen from 126 to 527, while the total figure jumped from 800 in 1987 to over 1000 in 1990 (Fig. 1.4). How much cocaine could this group realistically be consuming in a year? One detailed study of a representative sample of cocaine users defined heavy use among the sample as at least 3 g a day (Spotts and Shontz, 1980). One London street agency that sees a number of cocaine users indicates that a typical pattern of heavy cocaine use would be to use the drug on a daily basis for three or four days and then to rest before starting on another 'run' (Community Drug Project, London, 1991). Thus one could calculate that a heavy cocaine user consuming 3 g a day in four-day 'runs' per week could theoretically consume roughly 600 grams a year or just over half a kilo. Thus the 1000 notified users in 1990 could consume around 660 kg a year – about 10 per cent more than the total Customs seizures for the same year.

However, the statistics present us with a problem because it has been estimated for heroin that perhaps for every one user who is

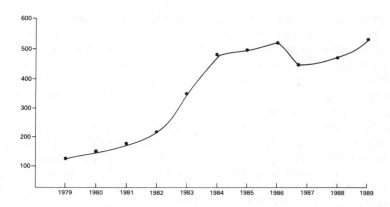

*Figure* 1.4   Numbers of new drug addicts notified to in the Home Office as being dependent on cocaine at time of notification, 1979–89

Source: *Home Office Statistical Bulletin*, issue 7/90, March 1990.

notified five are not (Hartnoll *et al.*, 1985), and there are reasons to believe that those with a cocaine problem are even less likely to come forward (see below). Thus even if one were to multiply the cocaine notification figures only by a factor of five, one has a potential cocaine consumption figure of at least 3000 kilos. Added to that would be an unknown figure for those who use the drug recreationally or occasionally. It should be said that in default of adequate research, the assumption here is that the pattern of cocaine use is similar to that of heroin, in that there is a known heavy-user group, a larger unknown heavy-user group and a much larger recreational group. However, given the widespread availability of amphetamine and the expense of cocaine, it is possible that in Britain the heavy cocaine user group is proportionally much smaller, with the main users of the drug being recreational or occasional consumers.

To try to ascertain the percentage of agency clients actually coming forward with a primary cocaine problem, 70 drug agency reports were surveyed from existing ISDD records. These comprised annual reports from individual agencies giving details of client contact and primary drug of use, and also small-area multi-agency studies where information had been collated from a number of different referral sources (for example, drug agencies, probation services, social services, GPs, and so on, on the basis of questionnaires. There are a number of drawbacks to information of this kind, such as the level of compliance from the reporting agencies in returning questionnaires, and double-counting, whereby one client is referred by more than one agency or presents more than once to the same agency. Though they were specifically concerned with the task of ascertaining the extent of cocaine problems, many reports did not differentiate between cocaine and amphetamine, merely listing these under 'stimulants'. In addition, it was often not possible to discern whether the figures related to cocaine mentions with another drug as the primary drug of misuse, and/or whether cocaine was a problem in addition to another main drug, such as opiates. Some agencies reported no referrals at all and very little local prevalence of cocaine use. However, taking all this into account, it was consistently clear that few agencies were seeing clients with a primary cocaine problem, and for those agencies that did see such clients, they represented no more than 1 per cent of the agency caseload. There were exceptions to this pattern; the client caseload for some agencies in the south London area and Manchester included a higher percentage than average of those presenting with a primary cocaine problem than reported in other parts of the country; around 10 per cent in one case. However, in terms of actual numbers of people, this still represented only a handful of individuals in a given year.

Interestingly, comments in those reports which took a broader view of the prevalence of drug use in their area (that is, comments which were not just single-agency based) were clearly aimed at challenging what may have been a distorted local media perspective on cocaine use in that area; for instance 'contrary to media propaganda, the cocaine industry would not appear to have arrived in Salford at present' (Polese, 1987) and from mid-Hampshire, 'there is little evidence to support the belief that cocaine is widely available or used in this area' (Harper, 1987). Other area reports did express some concern that cocaine was increasingly available, albeit from a very low base.

To see whether there had been any changes in the light of recent increases in seizures and notifications, phone-calls were made to ten key drug agencies around the UK, ensuring that there was a representative mix of all environments from rural to inner-city. The picture appears to be similar – some higher rates quoted in London and Manchester, but hardly any clients reporting primary use of cocaine; 'very, very, few' and 'hardly any' were typical remarks. Commenting on the cocaine notification figures for 1989, the Home Office observed,

The persistently small numbers of cocaine addicts notified (9 per cent) suggest that, despite seizures of cocaine by weight having exceeded those for heroin in 1987 to 1989, misuse of the drug has not so far resulted in significant demands for medical treatment. The only police force area with a high number of new cocaine addicts in 1989 was the Metropolitan Police Division with 270 addicts. No other area had more than 30. (Home Office, 1990)

It might be reasonable to assume that as cocaine is an expensive drug, those with the most problematic use are likely to come from the more financially secure sectors of society. Those from this group who are seeking help are more likely to present first to their own GP who might then refer them on to a private clinic or treatment centre rather than to a 'street agency' in the voluntary sector. To test out this theory, ten private establishments were also included in the telephone survey. Discussions with medical directors revealed that such centres are indeed seeing a higher number of clients with cocaine problems as a proportion of their client/patient group in a year – perhaps 4–10 per cent on average, with the higher figures coming once again from the London area. However, in absolute numbers, relatively few patients are seen with a primary cocaine dependency problem, although apparently there are several for whom cocaine is one drug problem among many (mainly heroin and alcohol).

Thus it could be that there is a far smaller cohort of heavy cocaine users in proportion to those for whom heroin is the major problem drug. However, even if this is correct, there are a number of reasons why those with an acute cocaine problem are less likely to present for treatment than, for example, heroin users. It could be that most people who use cocaine do not actually have a problem with the drug. Or it may be that users do not believe that cocaine is a drug that can cause problems and do not acknowledge as cocaine-related the problems they may be experiencing. But what about the person who is actively seeking advice or treatment? Historically, the drug agencies have been able to offer very little to stimulant users of any description, so there is little incentive for such a user to present for assistance (Standing Conference on Drug Abuse, 1989). Many drug users are understandably reticent about coming forward, for fear that making their drug use known will result in problems with the police, employers, and so on. Given that one of the symptoms of chronic cocaine use can be acute paranoia, one might conjecture that it is

hardly surprising that few heavy cocaine users are seen.
What about the prevalence of crack use? Certainly, agencies report
seeing even fewer 'crack clients', but interestingly, during the telephone survey, one agency in the Midlands said that although virtually
no crack users had presented themselves, agency staff had heard that
crack use was 'rife' in certain parts of Birmingham. Seizures of crack
have taken place in most of the UK's inner city areas, including
London, Liverpool, Manchester, cities in the West Midlands and
Cardiff.

One highly contentious issue is the prevalence of cocaine use
among the Afro-Caribbean community. Commentators are loath to
pursue this point for fear of exacerbating (largely) media portrayals
of cocaine use as a 'black drug problem'. Undoubtedly, there *is*
cocaine use among sectors of the British Afro-Caribbean population.
However, it has long been established that irrespective of the drug,
black drug users will not readily come forward to primarily white-run
street agencies or national health clinics (Awiah *et al.*, 1990; see also
Chapter 6) and it is likely that few are able to seek private treatment.

The literature-search for this chapter demonstrates an unknown
level of cocaine use by certain sectors of the black community, much
as it exists among sectors of the white population. One of the evaluation studies of the Government's anti-heroin campaign noted about
cocaine use, among those already using drugs, that 'there were signs
of increased trial (especially amongst blacks) and more general interest in trial' and quoted regular injectors from Cardiff as saying,
'There are a load of Rastas round here fixing smack and coke'
(Andrew Irving Associates, 1988); while a report from the Sheffield
area observed, 'Cocaine is beginning to appear in Afro-Caribbean
communities' (Drug Advisory Service, 1989). Young black males
who are part of the drug scene in Manchester are financing purchases
of expensive cocaine by dealing in other drugs. They also smoke
'crack', but refute the notion by saying that they are using 'washed
cocaine', suggesting perhaps that among this group, one's status is
demeaned by being dubbed a 'crack' user (North Western Regional
Drug Training Unit, 1991). This is not unlike the situation among
young people in south London during the craze for smoking heroin or
'chasing the dragon' in the early eighties. It was only a matter of
months for the label 'skag head' to be reduced from a heroic saluta-
tion to a term of abuse.

However, that cocaine use is far from being only a 'black problem'
is shown by the evaluation of the Riverside Community Drug Team

in West London conducted by the Centre For Research on Drugs and Health Behaviour. They too stated that 'early research suggested that cocaine use was concentrated within particular ethnic groups'. But later they described the three categories of drug users that they interviewed; one type was designated 'OC' or 'out of contact' with an agency for at least three months. This was the only group of the three that mentioned cocaine and, of 40 respondents, only 3 per cent were 'black British', the rest were either 'white British' or Irish and there were no Afro-Caribbeans (Power *et al.*, 1990).

In fact, there is a longstanding tradition in London of white stimulant use in areas of relatively high-density black population. The majority of illicit amphetamine in circulation during the sixties was diverted from pharmaceutical sources. However, as well as controlling this trade, the Krays and other criminal gangs also oversaw the limited East End production of illicit amphetamine for sale mainly to white youngsters in the West End clubs, many of whom lived in south London (Shapiro, 1989).

What about the prevalence of cocaine–crack use among other groups? There is evidence to show that, for a time, crack was used quite heavily by women working in the sex industries of large cities such as Liverpool and Birmingham (Matthews, 1990; Patel *et al.*, 1989) although heroin remains the primary drug among those within this group for whom drugs are a problem.

Among the general population there is a similar dearth of information. The literature-search included all surveys done of the school population. These are invariably conducted on the basis of self-reported questionnaires which, even when confidential, present the analyst with questions about honesty – the likelihood of 'boasting' or alternatively reticence about personal disclosure. Additionally, there is the problem of truancy; those who are consistently absent from school may (for a number of reasons) be those most liable to come into contact with drugs. However, it is clear from those surveyed that very few young people under 20 are even coming into occasional contact with cocaine. In a 1987 survey of young people in South Sefton, Liverpool, none of the 253 respondents admitted to trying heroin or cocaine or to having a close friend who had even tried these drugs once, while 91 per cent said they had never even been offered those drugs, the highest percentage for that question. Ninety-five per cent said they would never take it (Newcombe and O'Hare, 1988). A similar result was obtained from a survey of Wolverhampton schoolchildren – none of those surveyed had been offered cocaine (Wright,

1990). Higher 'exposure' figures were obtained in West Lothian, where five of 915 13–16-year-olds (0.5 per cent) said they had tried cocaine (West Lothian Drugs Education Project, 1988). School students in England, Scotland and Wales were the subject of a survey conducted by the Health Education Authority's Schools Health Education Unit. Here the highest contact figure was recorded among fifth-form boys, 2.2 per cent of whom said they had been offered cocaine (Balding, 1988). The survey was repeated in 1988 when the figure for this same group had risen to 3.9 per cent (Balding, 1989). Highest of all in terms of actual use to date was a survey in inner London of over 3000 schoolchildren where 1.9 per cent of respondents claimed to have used the drug with varying degrees of frequency from once to daily. 'Cocaine use has been considered negligible among school-age British population. This study shows that 2 per cent of schoolchildren have tried cocaine, more than one third of them repeatedly' (Swadi, 1988). It is conceivable that young people in certain areas of inner London might have a higher-than-average chance of coming into contact with cocaine and other illegal drugs. However, it is doubtful whether such results can be meaningfully extrapolated for the whole of the country.

Certainly, awareness of cocaine and crack has increased among young people. The Wolverhampton survey has been running quinquennially from 1969. In that year 15 per cent mentioned cocaine when asked what drugs are used by addicts. In 1989, that figure had risen to 80 per cent, with 8 per cent also aware of crack at a point early on in the year *before* press coverage of the topic (Wright and Pearl, 1990). The often-claimed notion that cocaine is not regarded as a dangerous drug is belied by the high numbers in the surveys cited above who recognise cocaine as a drug of addiction or who say they would never take it if offered. This is further supported by comments received about cocaine from young people in the 13–20 age range surveyed by another of the market research companies employed to evaluate the impact of the Government's anti-heroin campaign. Awareness of cocaine was almost 100 per cent across the four age groups in the 13–20 band, but only 5 per cent claimed to know anybody who had used it or said they had been offered it themselves and only 1 per cent claimed to have tried it. Cocaine was perceived as lying far closer to heroin than cannabis in terms of dangers; 'unhealthy', 'can kill' and 'don't want to die' were typical of the comments received. The figures for contact with and exposure to heroin were very similar to those for cocaine (Research Bureau Limited, 1988).

Those who are using cocaine from among the wealthier groups in society are unlikely to be the subject of user surveys, so reports are mainly of the anecdotal/confessional type. One researcher interviewed a woman drug user who had been a legal secretary in the City for some years and had a boyfriend working in the futures market; 'Lots of these characters are cokeheads', she said, 'it gives them confidence and keeps them hyped up and going. They earn so much money that they never get into real trouble with it. And there's always recuperation in a private clinic if they ever need it.' (Power, 1988). In the wake of a 1986 CBI report on drug abuse in industry, the *Daily Telegraph* reported the case of 'John' who had an annual income of £65 000 and allegedly spent £15 000 a year of it on cocaine. 'John' said, 'The City and advertising and television industries are riddled with cocaine. I know of people with responsibility for huge deals who cannot get by without it.' Eventually, 'John' spent two months in a private treatment centre and went on to become actively involved not only in Narcotics Anonymous, but also (because of his drink problem) in Alcoholics Anonymous (Doyle, 1986).

Given how little we know about the prevalence of cocaine and crack use in Britain, it is hardly surprising that there is even less information about the patterns of use and what we have is almost entirely anecdotal. However, we can make a few isolated comments about patterns of use.

In addition to the small area studies located by the literature-search, information was also supplied to the author by the North Western Regional Health Authority Drug Misuse Database (hereafter DMD). This data related to 109 users of cocaine referred during 1989 by a wide range of referral sources, but primarily local community drug teams. As with all 'indicator' information of this kind, it can only provide a window into the total picture of drug use in the wider community of any given area (Donmall, 1990).

Summarising from DMD statistics and other small-area studies, it would appear firstly that cocaine is rarely used with any regularity by those under 20 years of age. Among regular users, it is often used in conjunction with other drugs, especially heroin, and may be injected with heroin (speedballs). Possibly because those who became regular cocaine users were relatively experienced users of other drugs by the time of first use, the progression to injecting cocaine could be rapid. A 1988 survey of the Sefton Probation Drug Team revealed that most of the client group had not tried cocaine before the age of 21 but, when they did, over half were injecting it (Buchanan and Wyte, 1987).

The DMD data shows that of those cited as cocaine users, only 6 per cent of reports gave cocaine as the primary drug of choice; the rest were said to be using heroin as their main drug. Of course, it is possible that cocaine users were presenting as heroin users in order to obtain a prescription for sale, but more likely these figures confirm the thesis that very few primary cocaine users actually present to health and social work agencies.

Cocaine may be used to 'rev' up a user after a bout of heroin or tranquilliser use or, alternatively, these sedative drugs may be used to offset the cocaine 'rush'. Because of the price, cocaine is often regarded as an occasional 'treat' at the weekend by those users most likely to come into contact with agencies. However, it seems that cocaine would be much more popular if it was less expensive. The cocaine 'rush' is perceived as 'smoother' than that experienced with amphetamine and presumably also there is the hope that cocaine would be at a higher purity level than amphetamine which can be cut up to 90 per cent with adulterants. However, this hope may be forlorn; a survey of illicit drug use in the Portsmouth area noted that the price of cocaine was no indicator of purity, much of that currently available being heavily cut with amphetamine. Users knew this and it deterred purchase (Brown and Lawton, 1988).

At present, there is no hard evidence to suggest that crack is consistently attracting a different and/or younger market than cocaine powder, although this drug has been picked up in raids on large parties frequented by young people where cannabis, ecstasy and LSD have also been seized (Strang *et al.*, 1990). While non-users perceive a marked distance between cocaine and cannabis in terms of dangers, among users this does not necessarily seem to be the case. One dealer known to the Lifeline Project in Manchester has been supplying cannabis to middle-class 'professionals' in one of the more affluent parts of the city for over ten years. The dealer told one of the project workers that there had been a recent increase in demand for both cocaine and ecstasy from this cannabis-using group (North Western Regional Drug Training Unit, 1991). Cannabis and cocaine are both seen as social/recreational drugs, typical use of which in-volves sharing the drug with others in social settings (Murray, 1984).

These middle-class drug users living in Manchester are an example of an unknown number of users who are never the subject of surveys because they neither present for treatment nor come to the attention of the police. One study that did reach beyond agency contacts involved interviews with 92 cocaine users in Scotland contacted by 'snowballing'. This revealed them typically to be polydrug users who used cocaine infrequently: only four had used once a week or more in the past three months, despite previous periods of heavier use. Most were middle class and snorted the drug (Ditton J. *et al.*, 1991). In Toronto, Canada, researchers attempted to construct a profile of the 'typical' cocaine user out in the community. Using personal contacts and an advertising campaign, they interviewed 111 people over 21 who had used cocaine in the past three years and had been in employment for six of the previous twelve months prior to the study. They were surprised that over a third of respondents were women, but concluded that the 'typical' occasional/recreational user was an unmarried male aged 21–35, employed in a white collar occupation, who snorted less than half a gram no more than ten times a year either at home or at a friend's house (Erickson *et al.*, 1987).

To conclude, on the basis of the current research, the overwhelming number of cocaine seizures by the Metropolitan Police and the general distribution of wealth within the UK, the indications are that the greatest concentration of cocaine use in Britain is in London and the South East, although significant use in the wider community is anecdotally reported in other large conurbations such as Manchester and Birmingham. And even if the pattern of heavy cocaine use is not the same as that for heroin, it is likely that there is substantially more cocaine in circulation than is intercepted by the enforcement agencies. Relatively few primary users of cocaine present to agencies, compared with heroin users. Reasons for this may include lack of treatment options for heavy cocaine users and the heightened level of anxiety about making use known, consequent on heavy use of the drug. Epidemiological research in this area may be hampered by the fact that heavy or even frequent recreational use of the drug may be confined to a sector of society unavailable and/or unamenable to research scrutiny.

What of the future for cocaine in Britain? All the statistical evidence available indicates that cocaine use in Britain is on the increase. However, it is still the case that at present, the demand for stimulant drugs in this country is served primarily by home-produced cheap amphetamine sulphate and, more recently, ecstasy. In contrast, cocaine is much more expensive and, in most areas, harder to obtain. For this picture to change dramatically, there would have to be either a significant levelling-out of the price differential between amphetamine and cocaine, or a sustained and ultimately successful enforcement effort at cutting off supplies of amphetamine both internally and from abroad. Alternatively, there would have to be such an overproduction of cocaine in the producer countries that the drug was sold cheaply as a 'loss leader' in Europe to create a market large enough to challenge the current ascendancy of widely-available cheap amphetamine. Even if that did happen, amphetamine manufacturers might respond with new products of their own such as 'Ice' (smoke-able methylamphetamine). With the advent of a European free market in 1992, there will be pressure on enforcement agencies to relax border controls. Even so, none of the scenarios for a substantial increase in the overall consumption of cocaine and crack in Britain, likely to impact on drug services nationally, seems probable in the foreseeable future.

NOTE

The author would like to thank Jasper Woodcock, OBE, Director of the Institute for the Study of Drug Dependence, London and Dr Mike Donmall of the North Western Regional Health Authority Drug Research Unit for comments received during the preparation of this chapter.

REFERENCES

Andrew Irving Associates (1988) *DHSS: anti-drugs – AIDS campaign. Qualitative evaluation report* (London: Andrew Irving Associates).

Awiah, J., Butt, S., and Dorn, N. (1990) '"The last place I would go": black people and drug services in Britain', *Druglink*: 5 (5), pp. 14–15.

Balding, J. (1988) *Schoolchildren and Drugs in 1987* (Exeter: Health Education Authority Schools Health Education Unit).

—— (1989) *Young People in 1988* (Exeter: Health Education Authority, Health Education Unit).

Berridge, V. and Edwards, G. (1987) *Opium and the People: Opiate use in nineteenth-century England* (New Haven: Yale University Press).

Brown, C. and Lawton, J. (1988) *Illicit Drug Use in Portsmouth and Havant: A local study of a national problem* (London: Policy Studies Institute).

Buchanan, J. and Wyte, G. (1987) *Drug Use and its Implications: A study of the Sefton probation service* (Bootle: Merseyside Probation Service).

Community Drug Project, London. Personal communication 1991.

Ditton, J., Farrow, K. Forsyth, A. *et al.* (1991) 'Scottish cocaine users: healthy snorters or delinquent smokers?', *Drug and Alcohol Dependence* 28, pp. 269–76.

Donmall, M. C. (1990) *The Drug Misuse Database: Local monitoring of presenting problem drug use* (London: Department of Health).

Dorn, N. (1989) 'Reflections on Two Rand Reports' (review), *International Journal of Drug Policy*: 1 (3), p. 30.

Doyle, C. (1986) 'High flier downed by drugs', *Daily Telegraph*, 30 September.

Drug Advisory Service (1989) *Report by DAS on Services for Problem Drug Users provided by Sheffield Health Authority* . . . (Sutton: DAS).

Erickson, P. G., Adlaf, E. M., Murray, G. F. and Smart, R. G. (1987) *The Steel Drug: Cocaine in perspective* (Massachusetts: Lexington Books).

Gillman, P. (1990) 'Crack for sale', *Sunday Times Magazine*, 1 April, p. 36.

Harper, D. (1987) *Report of a Prevalence Study into the Nature and Extent of Problem Drug Taking in mid-Hampshire* (Winchester: Winchester Health Authority).

Hartnoll, R., Mitcheson, M., Lewis, R., and Bryer, S. (1985) 'Estimating the prevalence of opioid dependence', *The Lancet*: 1 (8422), p. 203.

Hewitt, C. (1987) 'A cocaine explosion?', *Druglink*: 2(2), p. 7.

Home Office (1990) *Statistics of the Misuse of Drugs: Addicts notified to the Home Office, United Kingdom, 1989* (Croydon: Home Office Statistical Division).

Home Office (1991) *Statistics of the Misuse of Drugs: Seizures and offenders dealt with, United Kingdom 1990*. Area tables (Croydon: Home Office Statistical Division).

Home Office Drugs Inspectorate (1990) *Cocaine and crack – update* (London: Home Office Drugs Inspectorate).

House of Commons Home Affairs Committee (1984–5) *Misuse of Drugs (Interim Report)*, HC 1984–1985, no. 399 (London: HMSO).

Johnson, E. M. (1987) 'Cocaine: the American experience', in Allen, D. (ed.), *The Cocaine Crisis* (New York: Plenum Press).

Matthews, L. (1990) 'Female prostitutes in Liverpool', in Plant, M. (ed.), *AIDS, Drugs and Prostitution* (London: Routledge).

Mirza, H. S., Pearson, G. and Phillips, S. (1991) *Drugs, People and Services: Final report of the drug information project to the Lewisham Safer Cities Project* (London: Goldsmiths' College).

Murray, G. F. (1984) 'The Cannabis–Cocaine Connection: A comparative study of use and users', *Journal of Drug Issues*: 14, (4), pp. 665–75.

National Drugs Intelligence Unit (1991) *Drug Seizures 1990* (London: NDIU).

Newcombe, R., and O'Hare, P. (1988) *A Survey of Drug Use among Young People in South Sefton, 1987* (Liverpool: South Sefton Health Authority).

North West Regional Drug Training Unit (1991). Personal communication.

Patel, A., Merrill, J., Vidyasagar, H., and Kahn, A. (1989) 'Cocaine and crack' (letter). *British Medical Journal*: 299, p. 856.

Polese, P. (1987) *Myths or Reality: Drug problems in Salford* (Salford: Community Drug Team).

Power, R., Jones, S., Dale, A. *et al.* (1990) *The Riverside Community Drug, Alcohol and HIV Team: An evaluation of year one* (London: Centre for Research on Drugs and Health Behaviour).

Power, R. (1988) 'Drug scenes', *New Society*: 83, (1314), p. 17.

Research Bureau Limited (1988) *Heroin Misuse Campaign Evaluation* (London: RBL).

Royal Canadian Mounted Police (1986) *Monthly Digest of Drug Enforcement Statistics*: 6 (8), p. 23.

*Searchlight* (1990) 'Drugs – why black people suspect the police', *Searchlight*: no. 184, pp. 18–19.

Shapiro, H. (1989) *Waiting for the Man: The story of drugs and popular music* (London: Quartet Books).

Spotts, J. V. and Shontz, F. C. (1980) *Cocaine Users: A representative case approach* (New York: The Free Press).

Standing Conference on Drug Abuse (1989) *Working with Stimulant Users: Report of a SCODA members' conference* (London: SCODA).

Strang, J., Griffiths, P., and Gossop, M. (1990) 'Crack and cocaine use in south London drug addicts 1987–1989', *British Journal of Addiction*: 85, (2), p. 193–6.

Swadi, H. (1988) 'Drugs and substance use among 3,333 London adolescents', *British Journal of Addiction*: 83 (8), pp. 935–42.

Wagstaff, A. and Maynard, A. (1988) *Economic Aspects of the Illicit Drug Market and Drug Enforcement Policies in the United Kingdom*, Home Office Research Study No. 95 (London: HMSO).

West Lothian Drugs Education Project (1988) *Annual Report 1986/87* (Livingstone: WLDEP).

Wright, J. D. and Pearl, L. (1990). 'Knowledge and experience of young people regarding drug abuse 1969–1989'. *British Medical Journal*: 300 (6717), pp. 99–103.

# 2 Cocaine and Crack within the 'British System': A History of Control

## H. B. Spear and Joy Mott

To many, United Kingdom drug control policy is enshrined in the so-called 'British System', which is usually regarded as synonymous with 'the supply of heroin to addicts'. The critical role of cocaine in the development of legislative controls, which are as stringent as in most other countries and fully in keeping with the United Kingdom's international obligations and domestic needs, is seldom recognised. Cocaine played no part whatsoever in the creation of the 'British System' and only a subordinate part in the much-publicised and much-misunderstood changes which were made to the 'system' in 1968. Apart from a brief period in the 1960s the difficulties which the misuse of cocaine has presented for the British have not arisen from excessive, injudicious or irresponsible prescribing, or supplying of the drug by medical practitioners.

Although the practice of chewing coca leaf in South America had been known for centuries, the active principle of the leaf, cocaine, was not isolated until 1860, some eight years before the passage of the Pharmacy Act, 1868 which, for the first time, regulated the sale of poisons and similar dangerous substances in this country. Under this Act it became unlawful for any person to sell or keep 'open shop' for retailing, dispensing or compounding poisons unless he was a pharmaceutical chemist, or to sell any poison unless the container was distinctly labelled. The Act did not apply to wholesale supplying or the direct supply of drugs by doctors to their patients. The poisons covered by the Act were listed in a two-part Schedule, the sale of those in Part I, such as arsenic and potassium cyanide, being subject to additional requirements that the purchaser had to be known to the seller, or introduced by someone known to him, and the sale had to be recorded in a register giving the date, the type and amount of poison sold and the purpose for which it was required by the purchaser and their signature. 'Opium and all preparations of opium or of poppies' were included in Part II, to which only the labelling requirements applied, while patent medicines, many of which were opium-based, were specifically excluded from the Act. This meant, in practice, that members of the general public could continue to buy opium preparations without hindrance.

As the words 'morphine' and 'cocaine' were not to be found in the Schedule to the 1868 Act, some commentators have concluded that these drugs did not become subject to any restrictions on sale until the Schedule was amended by the Pharmacy and Poisons Act, 1908. Both drugs were, in fact, covered by the inclusion of 'Alkaloids, all poisonous vegetable alkaloids and their salts' in Part I of Schedule A to the 1868 Act as the *Chemist and Druggist* saw fit to remind its readers on 27 July 1901. Supporting the Government's proposal to revise the Schedule, the *Chemist and Druggist* commented:

> of all the horrors that have been created during the past twenty years, cocaine-taking is probably the worst. The horror has grown in the face of the fact that cocaine is in the first part of the poisons Schedule, but that fact has never been exactly appreciated by retailers. More stringent attention to the matter is necessary.

An example of this 'horror' was reported in the *Chemist and Druggist* of 2 December 1899, in an account, first published in the *Glasgow Evening Times*, of a young chemist who had been obtaining quantities of cocaine from chemists in the southern districts of the city by tendering false prescriptions and, on occasion being unable to pay. His story was that, following a severe attack of toothache when serving his apprenticeship, he had been recommended 'to try a little cocaine'. He did so, and from that time had continued to take small quantities, until he became 'a slave to the cocaine habit', requiring 60 grains (3600 mg) a day before his craving was satisfied.

Apart from the gentle rebuke to those pharmacists with a less than adequate knowledge of the provisions of the 1868 Act, these comments confirmed how cocaine, not long since hailed as a 'wonder' drug, had dramatically fallen out of favour with the medical profession. The advocacy of cocaine for its therapeutic stimulant effects and as a cure for morphinism by Freud, as well as the discovery of its local anaesthetic properties by Koller in 1884, had been followed by a period when 'the pages of the medical journals were crammed with enthusiastic demonstrations of the uses of the drug; doctors flooded into print in its praise and each contribution purported to establish a different usage to which this wonder drug could be put'.[1, 2] Nor were the fatigue-reducing and restorative properties of the drug overlooked and various coca-based patent medicines and tonic wines became freely available.[3] But soon the medical profession began to question the use of cocaine in the treatment of morphine addiction and to appreciate the dangers which its prolonged use could bring. A similar volte-face had occurred in the United States where, as Musto[4] noted, the early approval of cocaine gradually changed to concern and eventually to fear of its side effects on the mind and behaviour of users. Medical journals and newspapers increasingly reported on persons whose careers and lives had been distorted and damaged by inordinate use of cocaine.

## THE POISONS AND PHARMACY ACT, 1908

The campaign by the medical profession and the Pharmaceutical Society against the unrestricted availability of all patent medicines, which focused attention on the number of deaths associated with the use of freely-available opium-based preparations such as chlorodyne and laudanum, eventually led to the appointment in 1901 by the Lord President of the Council of a Departmental Committee[5] with terms of reference:

> to devise a new and more scientific classification of poisons contained in both parts of the Schedule (to the 1868 Act) and to make such additions and alterations as the increased knowledge of pharmacology render expedient and to determine whether any further modifications of the law are required in the direction of relaxing the restraints upon the sale of certain scheduled substances or including others under some form of precaution.

The tragic deaths from cocaine poisoning of two young actresses in 1901[6] ensured that the future status of cocaine would receive special attention but in fact the Departmental Committee spent little time considering it[7] and readily accepted the suggestion of the Pharmaceutical Society that together with morphine, cocaine should be specifically named in the amended Schedule.[8] The Vice-President of the Society, Mr C. Bowen Allen, a chemist in Kilburn, appeared before the Committee and, when asked if there was any danger of persons becoming dependent on cocaine as a result of obtaining large quantities of cocaine lozenges, which contained small amounts of the drug, he replied,

Not through cocaine lozenges, but with regard to other preparations of cocaine I wonder the Legislature has not stepped in and prevented the sale of them for some considerable time. There is considerable iniquity going on in that direction.

Having aroused the Committee's interest, Mr Allen declined to elaborate on this 'iniquity', as it was a matter beyond the Committee's terms of reference![9] It was to be another fifteen years before evidence surfaced of any 'iniquity' involving cocaine sufficiently serious to exercise official minds.

The Pharmacy and Poisons Act, which received the Royal Assent on 21 December 1908, retained the controls of the 1868 Pharmacy Act while repealing Schedule A of that Act and substituting another, and also regulated the sales of certain poisonous substances contained, for example, in weedkillers and sheep-dips. The new Schedule included in Part I 'coca, any preparations or admixtures of, containing 1 or more per cent of the coca alkaloids' and, in Part II, 'preparations or admixtures containing more than 0.1 per cent but less than 1 percent of coca alkaloids'. The latter could be sold by persons approved by their local authority, while preparations containing less than 0.1 per cent remained free from any restriction on sale. The more potent preparations of cocaine were thus explicitly brought under the most stringent controls of the 1868 Act but the purchaser was still not required to present a doctor's prescription.

## DEFENCE OF THE REALM ACT, 1914, REGULATION 40B

Public concern about cocaine reached a high pitch in 1916 when it became apparent that it was being used and peddled by prostitutes in London and a number of cases were reported to the police in which the drug had been given to Canadian soldiers. Under the Defence of the Realm Act 1914 the gift or sale of intoxicants (an intoxicant being 'any sedative, narcotic or stimulant') to a member of His Majesty's Forces, with intent to make him drunk or incapable, was punishable by imprisonment up to six months, but the sale to, or possession of 'intoxicants' by civilians could not be satisfactorily dealt with under existing poisons law. A prosecution at Bow Street Police Court in May 1916 had failed on the magistrate's ruling that mere possession of cocaine was not an offence and the arresting officers had witnessed only an attempt to sell cocaine, rather than an actual sale.[10] A subsequent Army Council Order in May 1916 forbade the sale or supply of cocaine, and other drugs, to any member of the forces unless ordered by a doctor on a written prescription which could be dispensed only once.

But the Order had little effect on the non-medical trade as the drug was passed on to soldiers by prostitutes in circumstances under which it was virtually impossible for the police to intervene. In May 1916 Sir Edward Henry, the Commissioner of Police for the Metropolis, asked the Home Office to take urgent steps to close these loopholes and in a further letter[11] of 20 July 1916, following a number of convictions of dealers resulting from the use of a Canadian Military Police Sergeant as an undercover agent, he commented:

> To stamp out this evil, now rapidly assuming huge dimensions, special legislation is imperatively needed. I beg therefore to ask that the necessary powers may be obtained with the least possible delay, and I am desired to associate with me in this request the General Officer Commanding the London District with whom I have had grave conferences on the subject, and who sees in such a step alone the necessary protection for his troops in London. Great as is this need, however, in my judgement protective measures are not less needed in the interests of the civilian population, at present gravely menaced.
>
> I wish to urge to the utmost of my ability, that it will be of no value, in any restrictive measures, merely to deal with illicit sales; it is essential if the problem is to be seriously grappled with, that the unauthorised possession of this drug shall be an offence punishable, at least in certain circumstances, with imprisonment without the option of a fine.

In this letter Sir Edward made a number of specific practical proposals, most of which were included in the Defence of the Realm Regulation 40B, promulgated by Order in Council on 28 July 1916. His demand for substantial penalties for offenders prompted doubts in the Home Office about whether someone who had cocaine in his possession for his personal use should be liable to the same penalty as someone who had it in his possession to sell. (This doubt was eventually resolved by the creation of the offence of being in possession of a drug 'with intent to supply' under the Misuse of Drugs Act 1971.)

From July 1916 only 'authorised' persons: retail pharmacists, medical practitioners, persons holding general or special permits issued by the Secretary of State, or persons who had received the drug on doctors' prescriptions, were entitled to possess cocaine or preparations containing more than 0.1 per cent of cocaine. These were the limits under the 1912 International Opium Convention, the Hague Convention, which did not come into force until 1920. All transactions in the drug, including details of persons for whom it had been prescribed, on a prescription that could be dispensed once only, were to be separately recorded and these records could be inspected by anyone authorised for the purpose by the Secretary of State. At the same time a Proclamation under the Customs Consolidation Act 1876 prohibited the import and export of cocaine except under licence.

Regulation 40B was amended in December 1916 to give the Secretary of State power to issue licences for the manufacture of cocaine, to make it an offence for a medical practitioner to give a prescription for cocaine otherwise than in accordance with the conditions laid down in the Regulations, and to require medicines and other preparations containing cocaine to be marked with the amount of cocaine in them. The most important amendment, however, in view of its subsequent value in dealing with doctor addicts, was the power given to the Secretary of State to direct that an 'authorised' person who had been convicted of an offence against the Regulation, or Proclamation, should cease to be 'authorised'. In December 1916 Mr Anderson, a Home Office official, was empowered to inspect all books and records required to be kept under Regulation 40B, as it was thought there might be unspecified occasions when it would be advisable not to use the police. Similar authority was not extended to the police until May 1917, when, following a review by the Home Office of the operation and effects of Regulation 40B, it was decided to authorise 'all officers of police of a rank not below that of an inspector' to inspect the records.[11]

Before the war there had been much concern about the use of cocaine as an anaesthetic by unqualified dentists but a Departmental Committee on coroners in 1910 had not advised changes in legislation to prohibit their doing so.[12] A perhaps unforeseen consequence of the introduction of Regulation 40B was the public and political pressure which would be stimulated by the decision to allow only those 'unregistered' dentists who were in practice when the Regulation came into force, on 28 July 1916, to obtain preparations of cocaine containing more than 1 per cent of cocaine. As there were at that time, and likely to be for some time in the future, far more persons practising dentistry than were registered under the Dentists

Act, 1878, mainly in the working-class areas in the North of England, the restrictions imposed by Regulation 40B were interpreted 'in a directly anti-working class way'.[12] As a result of this pressure the Committee on the Use of Cocaine in Dentistry was appointed in November 1916, under the Chairmanship of Sir Charles Hobhouse, MP, and having as one of its members a future Prime Minister, Stanley Baldwin, MP. The Committee's terms of reference were to 'consider the authorisations for the use of cocaine in dentistry and to advise whether or not they should be continued or modified or if continued in what cases and within what conditions'.[13]

Much to the obvious irritation of Sir Malcolm Delevingne, then in charge of drugs matters at the Home Office, the Committee spent some time looking into the prevalence of the cocaine habit and, in addition to Sir Malcolm, invited evidence from Sir Francis Lloyd, the General Officer Commanding the London District, and from Sir Edward Henry, the Commissioner of Police for the Metropolis. The often vague and contradictory evidence which the Committee heard[14] provides an interesting insight into the cocaine 'epidemic' of that period.

In his evidence to the Committee, Sir Francis Lloyd expressed the view that the practice of using cocaine was 'exceedingly rife at the present time and probably worse than it has been. There has been no diminution of it since the Regulation' and he urged that continued restriction of use of cocaine was desirable, 'in the interest of the Army'. Sir Francis was accompanied by Sergeant Gilbert Smith of the Canadian Military Police, who, in an undercover role, had assisted the police in the arrest of a number of cocaine dealers. He told the Committee that cocaine in liquid form was being used by prostitutes before the arrival of the Canadian troops, whose main contribution had been to introduce them to the powder form. When asked to comment on the scale of the problem he said he had personally seen between 200 and 300 persons 'handling it', out of the 200 000–250 000 Canadian troops passing through London.

On the other hand, the view of the Metropolitan Police was that there had been 'a very marked diminution' since the Regulation came into force. The problem, which had first come to notice towards the end of 1915, was 'most prevalent among soldiers belonging to the Canadian contingent who introduced it to other soldiers and the prostitutes with whom they associated'. The main source of cocaine had been chemists' assistants in the West Central District of London and there was no evidence that unregistered dentists were in any way involved. The sale of the drug in London had now been practically stamped out, as a result of the inability to obtain supplies, as much as to any police effort, but it would be 'lamentable' if Regulation 40B was removed.

Sir Malcolm Delevingne's contribution, as he was obliged to admit, was largely negative. When asked if Regulation 40B had been effective, he replied that he had no evidence that it had broken down. The general opinion was that use of cocaine was spreading from the troops but there was no evidence of its extent among other classes, although medical men had told the Home Office that it existed. There was no trafficking in the drug among the working classes. The principal legitimate sources of cocaine, he believed, were Paris, Switzerland, the USA and possibly Holland but he could offer no information about the quantities of cocaine being imported under licence, as the licences were general and did not require this information to be specified. Neither had he received any reports of seizures of illicit supplies from Customs and Excise, although he had talked to officials of that Department.

If Sir Malcolm did not then have information about the quantities of cocaine imported into the UK, or perhaps for some reason was unwilling to provide it, it was certainly available. In 1920 the Home Office provided the League of Nations with details of cocaine imports, showing sources, and exports for the period 1911 to 1920.[15] Even though it was wartime, it is surprising that Sir Malcolm did not include Germany as a past, and potential if not current, supplier since that country's determination to protect its large cocaine manufacturing industry was one of the reasons for the delay in the ratification of the 1912 International Opium Convention. Nevertheless the implication, by Sir Charles Hobhouse and his colleagues, that Sir Malcolm was somewhat out of touch with the situation is a little unfair. The Home Office had only recently, and reluctantly,[16] become involved with the control of 'dangerous drugs' and had no machinery to provide such a senior official as Sir Malcolm with the rapid, widely-based assessments of drug-trends which are available nowadays from the Home Office Drugs Inspectorate, statisticians and research workers.

It is hardly surprising, in the circumstances, that the Committee came to the unanimous view that there was 'no evidence of any kind to show that there is any serious or perhaps even noticeable prevalence of the cocaine habit amongst the civilian or military population of Great Britain'.[13] Apart from his tetchiness at the Committee straying beyond its terms of reference by enquiring into the prevalence of cocaine misuse, Sir Malcolm was not best pleased that it had given unregistered dentists more than they had asked for. The Committee had recommended that any unqualified dentist, not just those who were in practice on 28 July 1916, who could satisfy his local authority, should be able to apply for registration for the right to purchase preparations containing not more than 1 per cent of cocaine. Before the Committee he had argued against any relaxation of the restrictions, not because unregistered dentists could not use cocaine safely but, because in his view, 'anyone could set up as an unregistered dentist' and any relaxation would therefore provide a channel for those wanting cocaine for illegitimate purposes.

However, Sir Malcolm need not have worried, as the Hobhouse Committee Report was overtaken by a new Committee, appointed to consider the regulation of the practice of dentistry and whose deliberations led to the Dentists Act, 1921. This decision was clearly welcomed in the Home Office where the file was minuted, 'It is fortunate there is so good a reason for not acting on the Committee's recommendations in the present circumstances'![17] Not only was there to be no extension of the right of unregistered dentists to obtain cocaine but the 1921 Act, which required the registration of all persons practising dentistry, enabled the existing exemption for unregistered dentists in practice on 28 July 1916 to be withdrawn.[18]

A further plea for permanent domestic legislation was made in February 1919, following the death, initially incorrectly attributed to cocaine, of a 22-year-old actress, Billie Carleton. The case prompted intense, and inevitably sensational, press coverage. In a letter of 4 February 1919,[19] the Director of Criminal Investigation at New Scotland Yard, Mr Basil Thomson, wrote,

In view of the undoubted growth of the drug habit, both in America and in this country and of the strong sentiment that the traffic should be brought under stricter control, the time seems to have come for enacting permanent legislation to take the place of Regulation 40B of the Defence of the Realm Regulations.

Mr Thomson's plea was timely, as the Government was about to honour its obligations under the International Opium Convention of 1912 (the Hague Convention) which had secured international agreement on the need to limit the use of opium, morphine and cocaine to 'legitimate purposes' and which had been ratified as part of the Versailles Peace Treaty. The Dangerous Drugs Act, 1920 and the subordinate Regulations which appeared the following year, not only extended control to morphine (which had been excluded from the provisions of Regulation 40B because in Sir Malcolm Delevingne's view 'morphine abuse was not nearly so serious or so urgent a matter' and would require 'different regulations'), but retained most of the provisions of Regulation 40B.

## THE DANGEROUS DRUGS ACT, 1920

It is doubtful whether the Dangerous Drugs Act, 1920, would have reached the statute book in the same form had the events of 1916, and the Billie Carleton case, not occurred. The early discussions on the legislation which would be required when the Hague Convention came into effect favoured an extension of the existing pharmacy laws, with increased professional self-regulation. Parsinnen[20] noted, 'the publicity which trailed in its (the Carleton case's) wake, stressing the depravity of drug-taking, made the public and politicians more willing to accept the stringent controls that were proposed in 1920.'

The Act prohibited the production, import or export, possession, sale or distribution of opium, cocaine, morphine or heroin except by persons licensed by the Home Secretary or otherwise authorised on that behalf and specified maximum penalties for offences under the Act. The prohibitions also applied to preparations containing 0.2 per cent of morphine or 0.1 per cent of cocaine. Conviction for an offence under the import and export prohibitions could involve the loss of the licence as well as the penalties imposed by the court. The Home Office, rather than the newly-created Ministry of Health, retained responsibility for 'dangerous drugs' and for the administration of the Act.

On 21 June 1922 Dr McDonald, MP, in a parliamentary question, asked the Minister of Health if he was aware that cocaine was not a drug essential to the medical and dental professions 'owing to the manufacture of less toxic substitutes' and if he would therefore take steps to prevent the importation of 'so pernicious a drug' into this country, if necessary by legislation. (This was the first, but certainly not the last, occasion on which the American prohibitionist approach to drug misuse was to be considered as a solution to the United Kingdom's drug problems.) The question was transferred to the Home Office, which replied that importation was already prohibited except under Home Office licence and that there would be consultations with the Ministry of Health about the first part of his question.

In due course, after taking soundings from the profession, the

Ministry of Health wrote to the Home Office, in a letter dated 17 July 1922, that cocaine was essential to medical practice, particularly as a local anaesthetic for use in opthalmic surgery and laryngology, and although dental surgeons were not unanimous, there was a large body of opinion to the effect that for certain dental operations cocaine was essential.[21]

In April 1923 the Minister of Health[22] appointed a Departmental Committee

> to investigate the comparative value, for therapeutic purposes for which cocaine is at present used, of various possible substitutes and the evidence as to risk, if any, of such substitutes becoming drugs of addiction.

The committee, on which the Home Office was represented by Sir William Wilcox, later to be a member of the Rolleston Committee, anticipated that their main work would be to investigate the merits of 'Butyn', a local anaesthetic developed in the United States. The 'organized opposition to substitution' from lately unregistered dentists was not anticipated. (The Dentists Act, 1921, required all current and future dental practitioners to be registered by the General Dental Council.) How this affected the Committee's work is unclear, because no report appears to have been published, but there could have been little doubt about the attitude of the medical profession to cocaine substitutes. Following a meeting of the Royal Society of Medicine in March 1924, when the question of substitutes was discussed, an editorial in the *British Medical Journal*[23] gave a clear warning that any attempt to deny medical practitioners the right to prescribe the drug of their choice would be opposed:

> While the medical profession is prepared to believe that the spread of the cocaine habit may have rendered it desirable to limit the legitimate use of cocaine as far as may be prudent or politic – since the smaller the legitimate use of the drug becomes the easier it will be to control the other uses – the proposal to prohibit medical practitioners from using a particular drug is open to serious objection, and it will be seen that the meeting last week was not prepared to pass a resolution affirming that cocaine should only be permitted to be used by the physician or surgeon himself and its prescription and dispensing abandoned.

In the event the warning was hardly necessary as the results of a comparison of the effects of cocaine, Butyn, tutocaine and other local anaesthetics by Copeland left little doubt of the superiority of cocaine in the treatment of certain conditions.[24]

The Cocaine Substitutes Committee is known to have held three meetings and to have set up two sub-committees. In a summary in 1924 of past experience they recorded their view that no substitute then available was capable of replacing cocaine 'for all purposes and on all occasions', that there were no known cases of addiction arising from the use of substitutes, and that the risk of establishing cocaine addiction from the legitimate medical use of cocaine was so small as to be practically negligible.[25]

What further conclusions the Committee reached are not known. When, in May 1930, Sir Malcolm Delevingne passed details of 'Percain' to the Ministry of Health he commented in his covering letter that he did not know if the Cocaine Substitutes Committee was still in being. Dr Smith Whitaker of the Ministry saw the approach as 'an opportunity to revive the Committee, explain why we have not called them together again and ask them to undertake this piece of work. Then we can present a report on results up to date and either ask for a standing committee, or wind up, perhaps handing the job over to the MRC'.[26] The absence of any international pressure to prohibit entirely the manufacture and use of cocaine, as there was in respect of heroin, probably explains why it is not possible to determine from the surviving official papers the ultimate fate of this Committee.


## THE ROLLESTON COMMITTEE, 1924–26

If cocaine played a critical role in the development of British drug control policy, even if the prospectus was false, it is important, in the present context, to note that it played no part whatsoever in the deliberations of the Departmental Committee on Morphine and Heroin Addiction (the Rolleston Committee) and the creation of the so-called 'British System'. Nor did cocaine have more than a subordinate role in the much publicised and much misunderstood changes which were made to that 'System' in 1968. The misuse of cocaine which had prompted the introduction of stringent controls in 1916 had not resulted from prescribed supplies and both the Army Council Order of May 1916 and Defence of the Realm Act Regulation 40B allowed for cocaine to be supplied on doctors' prescriptions. Neither order imposed any conditions on the circumstances under which such prescriptions could be issued but the Dangerous Drugs

Regulations, which came into force on 1 September 1921, limited a medical practitioner's authority to be in possession of, and to supply, drugs only 'so far as is necessary for the practice of his profession or employment in such capacity'.

This qualification soon led to differences of interpretation between the Home Office and the medical profession.[27] The basic question was whether the supply of drugs by a doctor to an addict was a proper exercise of that doctor's 'authority'. In 1924 the Ministry of Health appointed a Departmental Committee under the Chairmanship of the President of the Royal College of Physicians, Sir Humphrey Rolleston, 'to consider and advise as to the circumstances, if any, in which the supply of morphine and heroin to persons suffering from addiction to those drugs may be regarded as medically advisable . . .'.

The recommendations of the Rolleston Committee, from which the myth of the 'British System' derives, are well-known.[28] Put simply, the Committee accepted that any medical practitioner, in a genuine therapeutic relationship with someone who was addicted, could prescribe any drug to that person provided he was not merely pandering to their need for the drug. It is the effect which the Rolleston approach has, or has not had, on the overall British drug problem and its apparent abandonment in 1967 which attracts most controversy. This has been discussed in detail elsewhere[29] but the part played by cocaine in the events leading to the changes needs to be examined. That the prescribing of cocaine to addicts was not included in the Rolleston Committee's terms of reference, and did not arise during their enquiry, is understandable. By then the main therapeutic use of cocaine was as a local anaesthetic and the range of conditions requiring prolonged administration likely to lead to dependence, was very limited. None of the problem cases which had led to the appointment of the Committee had involved cocaine.

This was hardly surprising in the light of the reports from the police to the Home Office early in 1917 on the operation and effects of Regulation 40B. These disclosed that not only was there no evidence of the misuse of cocaine by soldiers or civilians in Birmingham, Bradford, Bristol, Cardiff, Hull, Leeds, Liverpool, Manchester, Newcastle, Sheffield or Southampton, but there had been such a marked reduction in the use and prescribing of cocaine that many chemists had ceased to hold stocks.[30] If there was little or no evidence of cocaine use in the provinces there was still, as Parsinnen[31] has shown, a problem in London, where 'it was in the hands of young street hustlers whose customers were prostitutes, actresses, criminals, well-to-do bohemians, night club habitués, and others on the fringes of London's underworld. They were fed by supplies from abroad and the activities of traffickers such as Brilliant Chang.'

The 1921 *Report to the League of Nations on Opium and other Dangerous Drugs* commented, 'it is clear that trafficking (in cocaine) still exists and it seems probable that it will not be possible to stamp it out until international co-operation in the control of the drugs has been fully established'.[32] Nevertheless, the Report for 1924 notes that the misuse of cocaine 'was on the wane',[33] a trend which was similarly apparent in the United States, where the New York City Mayor's Committee on Drug Addiction reported in 1930 that 'during the last 20 years cocaine as an addiction has ceased to be a problem'.[34]

The evidence the Rolleston Committee considered on the prevalence of addiction to morphine and heroin came almost exclusively from medical experience and it considered that 'this evidence has all tended in the same direction, and the collective effect is remarkably strong in support of the conclusion that, in this country, addiction to morphine or heroin is rare' and 'has diminished in recent years, most witnesses attributing the decline in the number of cases to the operation of the Dangerous Drugs Act which had made it more difficult to obtain the drugs otherwise than from, or through, doctors'. (If this was so it would not be unreasonable to assume addiction to cocaine was virtually non-existent.) Although sources of illegitimate supply existed, the Committee felt that 'those who might, in other circumstances, have obtained the drugs from non-medical sources are usually lacking in the determination and ingenuity necessary for overcoming the obstacles which the law now places in their way'.[35] This was a comforting and naive, if not entirely accurate, appraisal of the dynamics of drug dependence.

The principles for the treatment of addiction set out by the Rolleston Committee were applied to cocaine as well as to morphine and heroin, and twenty years later to the new synthetic narcotics such as pethidine and methadone. It was to be thirty years before the prescribing of cocaine to addicts, and then as a secondary drug to heroin, raised concern and for the touching optimism of the Rolleston Committee, that potential drug misusers would be unable to circumvent the statutory controls, to be shattered.

THE EXTENT OF COCAINE ADDICTION 1920–67

In reaching the conclusion that the use of cocaine as a recreational drug was on the wane by 1924, Parsinnen[36] relied mainly on prosecution statistics and the frequency with which the misuse of cocaine and other drugs were mentioned in the media. In 1921 there were 58 prosecutions for offences involving cocaine, of which 39 were for unlawful possession, and in 1927 there was only one. This led him to conclude that 'by 1930 narcotic drugs virtually disappeared from the newspapers, then from novels and films and finally from the public consciousness'. For the next three decades these same indicators, augmented by one which was not available for the 1920s, revealed a largely unchanged picture. After 1930, apart from a number of prosecutions in 1932 for 'technical' offences by pharmacists (failing to keep records, failing to keep dangerous drugs in locked cabinets), the five-yearly totals of prosecutions for offences involving cocaine did not exceed ten until 1961–65. (See Table 2.1.)

Although never slow to headline the drug elements in any story, even when, more often than not, they are little more than speculation and imagination, the press nevertheless provides an invaluable safeguard to official complacency. For example, in the early 1960s, a series of reports by Anne Sharpley in the *Evening Standard* drew attention to the misuse of amphetamines in the all-night clubs and coffee bars in the West End of London.[37] The press campaign she started led to the Drugs (Prevention of Misuse) Act, 1964, which brought amphetamines and later LSD under control. The absence of any sustained press interest in cocaine between 1930 and 1985, a period of over fifty years, strongly supports the official view that there was no widespread hidden problem.

In 1934 a new indicator, the number of addicts coming to the notice of the Home Office, became available. In that year the Home Office, responding to the growing interest of the League of Nations Opium Advisory Committee in the prevalence of addiction internationally, ventured the first estimate of the addict population of the United Kingdom.[38] The first Home Office Addicts Index also appears to have been started in that year, in which were recorded brief details of cases of addiction reported by Regional Medical Officers of Health, and cases, often involving doctors, discovered by Home Office Inspectors in the course of monitoring supplies from legitimate outlets, and some self-confessed addicts.[39] The first estimate was of an addict population of about 300, revised in 1935 to 700.[40] Thereafter, until

*Table* 2.1   Convictions for offences involving cocaine as a proportion of convictions for all offences involving controlled drugs, 1921–90

|         | Offences involving cocaine N | All offences N | Percentage of total involving cocaine |
|---------|------------------------------|----------------|---------------------------------------|
| 1921–25 | 239    | 871     | 27  |
| 1926–30 | 27     | 303     | 9   |
| 1931–35 | 29     | 302     | 10  |
| 1936–40 | 5(a)   | 154     | 3   |
| 1941–45 | 3(b)   | 1 104   | 0.3 |
| 1946–50 | 10     | 748     | 1   |
| 1951–55 | 6      | 972     | 0.6 |
| 1956–60 | 6      | 861     | 0.7 |
| 1961–65 | 14(c)  | 4 152   | 0.3 |
| 1966–70 | 499(c) | 37 865  | 1   |
| 1971–75 | 1 221  | 63 897  | 2   |
| 1976–80 | 1 791  | 70 762  | 3   |
| 1981–85 | 2 885  | 113 917 | 3   |
| 1986–90 | 3 204  | 164 035 | 2   |

*Sources*
1921–45   Annual Reports to the League of Nations by His Majesty's Government in the United Kingdom on 'The traffic in opium and other dangerous drugs'.
1946–70   Annual Reports to the United Nations.
1971–89   Home Office Statistical Department.
1990      Home Office Research and Statistics Department.

*Notes*
1. From 1921 to 1970 the statistics refer to the number of convictions excluding technical offences (e.g. pharmacists not keeping a register, etc). From 1970, the statistics refer to the number of persons found guilty or cautioned or when the offence was settled by HM Customs and Excise by compounding, i.e. the payment of a penalty in lieu of prosecution.
2. The number of prosecutions for offences involving cocaine are not separately available for:
(a) 1939.
(b) 1940–1943.
(c) 1965 and 1966.
3. The total number of convictions for 1964 to 1970 include prosecutions brought under the Drugs (Prevention of Misuse) Act 1964.

1968, when the procedure for doctors to notify their addict patients to the Chief Medical Officer at the Home Office was introduced, the statistics related to the number of addicts 'coming to the notice of the Home Office' each year.

It must be admitted that these statistics were of limited value as an indicator of the prevalence of addiction since the arrangements for bringing cases to notice can only fairly be described as primitive. Then, as now, addicts obtaining their drugs entirely from illicit sources were unlikely to come to official notice nor were some who were supplied by licit sources. The police, who in 1921 had been given the responsibility for monitoring retail pharmacies, were not asked until 1939 to report individuals receiving regular or unusual supplies to the Home Office for further enquiry. It was not until the early 1980s that the reporting of such supplies reached acceptable standards when there were specialist officers to carry out this task in most police forces. Another factor that distorted the statistics was the practice, not changed until 1945, of retaining addicts' cards in the Index for ten years after the last information about them was received, except, of course, in the case of death; from 1945 onwards cards were to be retained for only one year but there is some doubt that this was strictly adhered to, and it is probable that the Index continued to include as 'active' some addicts about whom there was no recent information.

Nevertheless, it is interesting to note that the 1935 estimate of 700 addicts was not to be exceeded until 1964 by which time there were other clear signs that addiction was a growing problem.[41] The absence of such signs during the previous thirty years together with the official addict statistics, whatever their shortcomings, enabled the Government to report regularly to the League of Nations that 'drug addiction is not prevalent in Great Britain', and later to the United Nations, that 'cases of heroin and cocaine addiction are now comparatively rare'. Such statements were, not surprisingly, viewed with some scepticism in some countries with more serious problems, as the United Kingdom delegate to the United Nations, T. H. Hutson,[42] commented in March 1949:

> It is of particular note that the UK remains astonishingly free from illicit traffic in drugs as compared with the USA and Canada, for instance. The representatives of those countries always say (in private) that we are damned hypocrites and that we have far more than we own up to. But it is an inexplicable fact none the less; I

don't know what to attribute it to, except that in a deep seated way the country remains law abiding.

If the overall drug-addiction picture gave no cause for official or public concern, the situation in relation to cocaine was even more satisfactory. The 1947 Report to the United Nations[43] gave a figure of 383 addicts known to the Home Office and, while not specifying the number of known cocaine addicts, included the comment:

A few addicts use cocaine but the number addicted to this drug tends to diminish with the passing of time. Fresh cases of addiction to cocaine are rare. During the year it became evident that Pethidine must be regarded as a more usual drug of addiction than cocaine now is.

As with those addicted to morphine or heroin, the majority of the cocaine addicts of this period were of therapeutic and quasi-therapeutic origin, ranging from the opera singer whose dependence resulted from the prolonged use of a prescribed throat spray containing cocaine, to the doctor who had first been introduced to cocaine around the turn of the century by a personal physician to the Kaiser and who was still receiving about 600 mg per day at his death within sight of his 100th birthday!

There were, however, a small number of recreational morphine and heroin addicts who were also using cocaine but who posed few problems, being supported mainly, and occasionally generously, by prescriptions, supplemented from time to time with illicit imports of heroin and the proceeds of theft from wholesale or retail chemists. In the main they were from the higher social and economic levels with relatively high intellectual achievements, having taken drugs originally 'in order to live more fully'.[44] There was a certain amount of borrowing and lending of drugs between these addicts, whose main social contacts were at commonly-used pharmacies and doctors' surgeries. There was little evidence of the widespread selling of surplus supplies, a practice which was to cause difficulties over the next few years, although the most notorious addict of the period, who in the years before her death in 1959 was receiving about 4000 mg of cocaine daily, was certainly not averse to 'sharing' her supplies with others. (The only member of the new group of heroin addicts to have come to notice before the events of 1951 described below, admitted he was first introduced to cocaine by this addict, and was content for some years to exchange some of his own prescribed heroin for some of her cocaine, rather than try to persuade his doctor to prescribe him cocaine.)

The emergence of a new group of heroin addicts, differing in many respects (in age, social status and interests) from the prewar addicts, has been discussed in detail elsewhere[41] but less attention has been paid to the part played by cocaine in the evolution and development of this group and in the events leading to the 1967 changes to the 'British System'. The origins of this new group can be traced with reasonable accuracy to 1951, when most of the heroin and cocaine which had been stolen from a hospital in Kent was successfully disposed of in the West End of London before the culprit, Kevin Patrick Saunders ('Mark') a porter at the hospital, was arrested. Saunders' activities resulted in the appearance of a number of previously unknown heroin addicts who approached doctors for 'treatment' but surprisingly none sought or were given supplies of cocaine. Signs of a revival of interest in cocaine had appeared a year earlier. In April 1950 during a Metropolitan Police raid on 'Club Eleven', a modern jazz club in Carnaby Street, three men, one of whom was to come to notice as a heroin addict, were found to be in possession of cocaine which had been adulterated with boric acid. No heroin was found but the police did recover one empty morphine ampoule from among the packets of Indian Hemp (as cannabis was then known) discarded on the floor.[45]

The credit for reintroducing cocaine to the 'British System' must go to a Nigerian addict who in January 1954 approached a young general practitioner, with no known previous connection with addicts, with the story that he had just returned from the United States where he had been studying law and had become addicted to heroin. By the end of the month he had persuaded the doctor to add cocaine to the lavish supplies of heroin he was prescribing, on the grounds that cocaine would help him cut down his heroin intake. Within a short time, two other Nigerian addicts had successfully persuaded their doctors that they needed cocaine and prescriptions for both heroin and cocaine became a more frequent sight in West End pharmacies. Although there is no doubt that the first of this trio was addicted to both heroin and cocaine, there is equally no doubt that he sold a substantial proportion of his prescribed supplies, as was shown by the dramatic deterioration in his lifestyle when his original prescriber was persuaded to withdraw and he was forced to find another doctor, who proved to be far less gullible and generous.

In 1958 the Ministry of Health and the Department of Health

for Scotland appointed an Interdepartmental Committee on Drug Addiction, under the chairmanship of Sir Russell Brain, to:

> review in the light of more recent developments, the advice given by the Departmental Committee on Morphine and Heroin Addiction in 1926; to consider whether any revised advice should also cover other drugs liable to produce addiction or to be habit forming; to consider whether there is a medical need to provide special, including institutional, treatment outside the resources already available, for persons addicted to drugs. . . . .

The Committee reported in 1961 and did not recommend any changes to the principles of treatment for addiction set out by the Rolleston Committee, concluding that 'the incidence of addiction to drugs controlled under the Dangerous Drugs Act 1951, is still very small and the traffic in illicit supplies is almost negligible, cannabis excepted'.[46]

There were already signs of the renewed interest in cocaine in the addict statistics considered by the Committee, although few doctors were then prepared to prescribe it. At a meeting of the Society for the Study of Addiction in April 1961, when Sir Russell Brain gave a preview of the report, a pharmacist working in the West End of London suggested that the Committee had underestimated the extent to which illicit supplies of heroin and cocaine were available.[47] The Reports to the United Nations show that, in 1957, of the 359 addicts known to the Home Office 16 (4 per cent) were using cocaine, rising to 30 (7 per cent) of 454 in 1959, with the proportion continuing to increase thereafter.[41] The increase was very largely due to the entry into the addiction-treatment field of Lady Isabella Frankau, a psychiatrist in private practice, whose generous prescribing of both heroin and cocaine was to lead, in 1964, to the reconvening of the Interdepartmental Committee. This ground has also been well traversed[29] but hitherto interest has focused on her prescribing of heroin, while the rationale for her treatment, which included prescribing cocaine, has received less attention.

In 1960 Lady Frankau[44] described her treatment programme as involving, as a first phase, the stabilisation of the patients' intake of heroin and cocaine by prescribing 'adequate supplies' in order to free them morally and financially from the 'degradation and humiliation' of reliance on drug pedlars and the black market and to make it easier for those who could, to work. The second phase involved cutting down the doses of heroin and cocaine and adding benzodiazepines to control their anxiety and sleeplessness, with vitamins to improve their physical state, and eventually, in-patient withdrawal.

Nowhere are the contradictions which characterised Lady Frankau's approach to the treatment of addiction more apparent than in relation to cocaine. It is clear that she recognised the very strong hold which cocaine exerted on those who took it regularly, and the difficulty of reducing the dosage, let alone withdrawing the drug completely, yet within a short time she was prescribing cocaine to heroin addicts who had not previously used it. Many of the veteran Canadian addicts who became her patients in the early 1960s complained that they experienced no 'high' from the pharmaceutically pure heroin they were receiving on her prescriptions. In an attempt to recapture that sensation she arranged for them to be supplied, for a time, with mixtures of heroin and some of the adulterants found in illicit heroin in Canada, and later with cocaine, which, as the Canadian authorities were quick to inform the Home Office, they had never had in Canada. There was no mention of cocaine in a paper on the treatment of Canadian addicts she contributed to the *Canadian Medical Association Journal* in 1964.[48]

When describing her treatment programme[44] she noted:

although cutting down the amount of cocaine produced no withdrawal symptoms any suggestion of reducing the dose was met by resistance and even violent reactions. Fantastic stories were offered in efforts to obtain extra cocaine, but the most common pretexts were 'accidents' which happened while they were preparing the cocaine for injection. They also pleaded that if only the cocaine could be increased, then they would find it easier to cut down on the heroin.

In practice, however, she rarely if ever reduced the heroin dosage and not infrequently increased it as well as the dosage of cocaine.

The small number of other doctors in London who treated heroin addicts also began to prescribe them cocaine 'because Lady Frankau told us to'.[49] The consequences of this treatment policy was reflected in the rapid rise in the number of cocaine addicts coming to the notice of the Home Office. Examples of Lady Frankau's prescribing, such as the six-week supply of 10 grains of heroin and 15 grains of cocaine to an addict who, three days later, using another name, became a patient of another doctor who prescribed further supplies, ensured that the prescribing of cocaine would be included in the terms of reference of the reconvened Interdepartmental Committee on Drug Addiction in 1964.

The Interdepartmental Committee, again under the chairmanship of Lord Brain, was reconvened in July 1964, to consider whether, in the light of recent experience, the advice they gave in 1961 in relation to the prescribing of addictive drugs by doctors needs revising and, if so, to make recommendations.

The Committee learned that the number of addicts known to the Home Office had risen from 454 in 1959 to 753 in 1964, that the number of cocaine addicts had increased from 30 to 211 with virtually all the new cocaine addicts using heroin as well, that the proportion of non-therapeutic addicts had risen from 22 per cent to 49 per cent, and the proportion of addicts aged under 35 had risen from 11 per cent to 39 per cent, with 40 aged under 20 in 1964. The increase in addiction to heroin and cocaine was largely centred in London but with indications of a similar trend on a smaller scale in one or two provincial cities.[50]

The Committee concluded that the major source of supply of heroin and cocaine to the addicts 'had been the activities of a very few doctors who had prescribed excessively for addicts . . . these doctors have acted within the law and according to professional judgement'. (In her evidence to the Committee in December 1964 Lady Frankau commented 'I never give cocaine if I can avoid it'!) The Committee 'remained convinced that the doctor's right to prescribe dangerous drugs without restriction for the ordinary patient's needs should be maintained' but the facility for addicts 'to obtain drugs legally has now been abused with the result that addiction has increased'.

In order to 'prevent abuse without sacrificing the basic advantages of the present arrangements' the Committee recommended:

(a) a system of notification of addicts;
(b) the provision of advice when addiction is in doubt;
(c) the provision of treatment centres;
(d) the restriction of supplies to addicts.

Since cocaine was used in ENT surgery the Committee declined to recommend that it should be totally banned.

## THE DANGEROUS DRUGS ACT 1967

The 1967 Act implemented the main recommendations of the Inter-departmental Committee. Regulations came into force on 22 February 1968 requiring doctors to notify to the Chief Medical Officer at the Home Office those of their patients who were addicted to any of the drugs controlled by Part 1 of the Schedule to the Dangerous Drugs Act, 1965 (covering drugs controlled by the 1961 UN Single Convention). Administrative action provided for the setting up of National Health Service drug-treatment centres, and Regulations came into force on 16 April 1968 which restricted the prescribing of heroin and cocaine to addicts to specially licensed doctors, most of whom worked in the treatment centres.

The restrictions on prescribing was the last occasion on which major control measures were specifically targeted at cocaine. The new arrangements effectively dealt with the problem which Lady Frankau's prescribing had created, as the treatment-centre doctors rapidly discontinued the prescribing of cocaine. By the end of 1969 only 81 addicts were still receiving cocaine on prescriptions.[51]

But, as the prescribed use of cocaine by addicts decreased, it became apparent that its use amongst the 1970s 'jet set', the equivalent of the 'yuppies' of the 1980s, was increasing and that this was part of a worldwide revival of interest in cocaine. From 1970 the conviction, seizure and notification statistics all began to show increases in respect of cocaine. But perhaps the most revealing indication of how popular cocaine was becoming was provided by a London doctor who asked if he was required to notify all the cocaine addicts he met socially! The most important difference between this new generation of cocaine misusers and those who preceded them fifty years earlier was that the cocaine they sniffed, or 'snorted', often through rolled-up banknotes, had been illicitly produced in South America and smuggled into this country.

After 1916, and with the success of Defence of the Realm Regulation 40B in closing the sources of supply in the United Kingdom, much of the cocaine available in the West End of London in the early 1920s came from Germany where, 'because of lax controls, and a large cocaine manufacturing industry' it could be easily obtained.[52] But as international controls were tightened, particularly by the 1931 International Convention for Limiting the Manufacture and Regulating the Distribution of Narcotic Drugs, which imposed manufacturing quotas on individual countries, this loophole was closed. It was not until the mid-1960s that economic and social changes in the South American producer countries, together with pressures from the United States to prohibit licit production, led to increases in the illicit production and export of cocaine.[53]

## THE MISUSE OF DRUGS ACT, 1971

Unlike the 1967 Dangerous Drugs Act, this Act was not introduced in response to any specific domestic problem. It was a consolidating measure and, while retaining the pattern of control established by earlier legislation, made more extensive and flexible provision for controlling drugs in order to prevent their misuse. The drugs controlled are now classified according to their perceived harmfulness, and the broad principle governing penalties for offences under the Act is that the most severe relate to trafficking offences and, in general, are graded in accordance with the harmfulness of the drug concerned, so that offences involving Class A drugs (including cocaine, heroin, and morphine) attract the most severe penalties.

## TACKLING DRUG MISUSE, 1984

The revival of interest in cocaine in the 1970s, and signs of the increased use of heroin, initially had little impact on the public and political consciousness, and it was not until the 1980s that 'the drug problem' again attracted sustained media attention. The trigger, however, was not cocaine but an explosion of heroin smoking on Merseyside and in some other inner-city areas.

In 1984 the Government's response was a five-point strategy for tackling drug misuse, in which a high priority was given to the more effective manning of the legislative defences already in place under the Misuse of Drugs Act, 1971. The strategy includes the reduction of supplies of drugs from abroad, increasing the effectiveness of enforcement, maintaining effective deterrents and tight domestic controls, developing prevention and education, improving treatment and rehabilitation. With one exception, none of the initiatives which were set in motion, and which are described in the various editions of *Tackling Drug Misuse*,[54] have been aimed specifically at cocaine. Heroin was 'the greatest menace' although the threat posed by other drugs, such as cocaine and amphetamines, and the importance of intravenous injection of drugs as a significant route to AIDS infection, were recognised.

Further legislation has been introduced to deter drug traffickers by increasing maximum penalties and by depriving them of the profits of their crimes. The maximum penalty for drug trafficking had been set at ten years' imprisonment by the Dangerous Drugs Act, 1923, when, with evidence of an outbreak of cocaine use in London, there were demands in Parliament and the press for heavier penalties than were originally provided in the 1920 Act. In 1984 this penalty was felt to be inadequate for offenders who had been convicted of trafficking in drugs worth millions of pounds and the Controlled Drugs (Penalties) Act, 1985, which came into force on 16 September 1985, increased the maximum penalty for trafficking offences to life imprisonment. The Drug Trafficking Offences Act, 1986, which came into force on 12 January 1987, provides comprehensive powers for tracing, freezing and confiscating the proceeds of drug trafficking, and measures to combat the laundering of illegal drugs money. This Act also contains provision for the enforcement in England and Wales of orders made by courts in designated countries for the recovery of the proceeds of drug trafficking and provides the basis for reciprocal agreements with other countries, with a view to the enforcement there of orders made in this country against assets held by convicted traffickers and vice versa.

The initiative mainly directed at cocaine was the inclusion of a clause in the Drug Trafficking Offences Act, 1986, making it an offence to sell or supply any article, except hypodermic syringes, which could be used or adapted for use in the administration of a controlled drug. This had been prompted by the discovery that cocaine kits were on sale in London.

Before the 'coherent and comprehensive' strategy for tackling drug misuse could begin to produce results it was necessary to improve, and in some instances to create, the machinery by which the objectives might be met. This was particularly true in the field of enforcement. In 1984, in order to enhance drug enforcement, the Association of Chief Police Officers set up a working party to review the arrangements within forces and the structure of Regional Crime Squads, and it was not until 1 January 1985 that all police forces in England and Wales had drug squads.[55]

The 1980s response to drug misuse differed from that of the 1920s in one important respect. In the 1920s the drug-taker was seen very much as a victim of the drug, his own lifestyle and more particularly of the drug dealer, and the most effective response was seen as strict enforcement and the imposition of salutary sentences by the Courts (see Table 2.2). The significance of the 'demand' for drugs and the need for the early identification of those at risk, were not recognised by the legislators of that period but since 1984 have been vital elements in the Government's strategy; for example, the drug prevention initiative set in train by the Home Office in 1990.[56]

*Table 2.2*  Sentencing of persons convicted of unlawful possession of cocaine, 1921–25 and 1986–90

|      | Convicted N | Imprisoned N | Imprisoned % |      | Convicted N | Imprisoned N | Imprisoned % |
|------|-------------|--------------|--------------|------|-------------|--------------|--------------|
| 1921 | 36*         | 33           | 92           | 1986 | 299         | 82           | 27           |
| 1922 | 51          | 48           | 94           | 1987 | 303         | 75           | 25           |
| 1923 | 42          | 29           | 69           | 1988 | 322         | 48           | 15           |
| 1924 | 15          | 11           | 73           | 1989 | 436         | 77           | 18           |
| 1925 | 6           | 2            | 33           | 1990 | 517         | 63           | 12           |

* Includes unknown number of unlawful import offences.

*Sources*
1921–25  Annual Reports to the League of Nations.
1986–90  Home Office Statistical Department, *Statistics of the Misuse of Drugs in the United Kingdom.*

## CRACK

The absence so far of any reference to 'crack' is deliberate because it has no place within the 'British System' since it is not a pharmaceutical product. Crack is simply the base alkaloid of cocaine, instead of the more frequently encountered salt, cocaine hydrochloride, and has been known as 'freebase' since the 1970s. Freebase cocaine or crack melts and then vaporises when heated by a direct flame and the inhaled vapour has an extremely rapid effect on the brain. As Edwards and Strang[57] neatly observed, 'crack is not a new drug but a new delivery system'. The existing legislation provides for penalties to deter the illicit importation, manufacture, production, supply, possession of cocaine in any form as well as the use of premises on which freebase cocaine is produced or supplied.

In 1989 there was much public anxiety in this country about the misuse of cocaine and crack. In April of that year Robert Stutman, then an agent of the United States Drug Enforcement Agency, in a missionary address to the Annual Drugs Conference of the Association of Chief Police Officers, which was attended by the then Home Secretary, Douglas Hurd, MP, predicted 'that in two years from now you will have a serious crack problem . . . we are so saturated with cocaine in the United States . . . it's got to go somewhere and where it is coming is right here'.[58] Following Stutman's largely anecdotal and unsupported statements there was a period of sensational press reporting about crack[59] leading Dorn to comment, 'the publicity sparks in every bored and impressionable drug user the idea of using and dealing in these stimulating commodities. Dealers are told that they can make a fortune, and that crack is the world's greatest hit. More people seek out cocaine, pop it in the microwave with a few easily obtained chemicals, and hey presto, there is an enlarged pool for the police to fish in'.[60] (See also Chapter 4.)

The House of Commons Home Affairs Committee, reporting in July 1989, after a visit to the United States, described crack as 'the single most addictive and dangerous form of drug abuse . . . more addictive and more damaging in its effects on society than any previously known drug of abuse . . . it can be almost instantly addictive . . . and can take over a person's life in under a week . . . above all crack leads to violent crime'. The Committee referred with concern to 'recent evidence from the National Drugs Intelligence Co-ordinator that crack misuse is an escalating problem, and one which . . . is spreading into the shire counties of England'.[61]

There can be little doubt that illicit supplies of cocaine are increasingly becoming available in the United Kingdom. In 1990 a record quantity, 610 kg, of cocaine were seized, with HM Customs seizing 90 per cent of this amount, with 69 seizures involving quantities of one kg or more compared with 54 in 1989. The number of seizures of cocaine, mainly by the police, had increased from 829 in 1988 to 1805 in 1990 including 320 (20 per cent) of crack.[62] During 1990 17 755 addicts were notified to the Chief Medical Officer at the Home Office of whom 1085 (6 per cent) were reported as addicted to cocaine and usually also to heroin, with 286 (2 per cent) reported as addicted only to cocaine.[63]

Whether the misuse of cocaine or crack escalates to the extent that has been feared, and it is to be hoped that it does not, will depend less on the introduction of new controls than on the effective implementation of those already in place and the success of the Government's general strategy against all forms of drug misuse.

## REFERENCES

1. Berridge, V. and Edwards, G. (1987) *Opium and the People* (New Haven and London: Yale University Press), p. 220.
2. *Chemist and Druggist*, 15 January 1885, pp. 33–7.

3. Berridge, V. and Edwards, G., op. cit., p. 221.
4. Musto, D. (1991) 'Illicit Price of Cocaine in Two Eras: 1908–14 and 1982–89', *Pharmacy in History*, 33, pp. 3–10.
5. Privy Council (1903) *Report of the Departmental Committee to Consider Schedule A to the Pharmacy Act 1868. Part I: Report*, Command 1442.
6. *Chemist and Druggist*, 27 July 1901, p. 151.
7. Privy Council (1903) *Report of the Departmental Committee to Consider Schedule A to the Pharmacy Act 1868. Part II: Minutes of Evidence and Appendix*, Command 1443. Appendix V includes a table showing deaths from poisoning for 1899 when there were 155 deaths (of which 69 were suicides) associated with the use of opium, morphia or laudanum, 12 (of which 3 were suicides) from chlorodyne and 1 suicide from cocaine.
8. Pharmaceutical Society of Great Britain (1901) Letter dated 5 December from the Registrar to the Secretary of the Poisons Committee.
9. Privy Council (1903) op. cit., Part II, Minutes of Evidence paras 788, 789.
10. Parsinnen, T. M. (1983) *Secret Passions, Secret Remedies* (Manchester: Manchester University Press), p. 131.
11. Public Record Office: HO 45/10813/312966.
12. Berridge, V. (1978) 'War Conditions and Narcotics Control: The Passing of Defence of the Realm Act Regulation 40B', *Journal of Social Policy*, 7, pp. 285–304.
13. *Report of the Committee on the use of Cocaine in Dentistry* (1917) Command 8489.
14. Public Record Office: HO 45/11013/323566.
15. *Report by the British Government to the League of Nations for 1920 on Opium and other Dangerous Drugs*.
16. Berridge, V. (1978) op. cit., p. 292.
17. Public Record Office: HO 45/11013/323566.
18. *Report by the British Government to League of Nations on Opium and other Dangerous Drugs, 1922*.
19. Home Office Papers.
20. Parsinnen, T. M. (1983) op. cit., p. 136.
21. Public Record Office: HO 45/19427/434228.
22. Ministry of Health, Cocaine Substitutes Committee. Public Record Office: MH 58/273.
23. *British Medical Journal* (1924) 22 March p. 535.
24. *British Medical Journal* (1924) 12 July.
25. Public Record Office: MH 58/273.
26. Public Record Office: HO 45/18469/537258.
27. Berridge, V. (1984) 'Drugs and Social Policy: The establishment of Drug Control in Britain 1900–1930', *British Journal of Addiction*, 79, pp. 17–30.
28. *Report of the Departmental Committee on Morphine and Heroin Addiction* (1926) London: HMSO (The Rolleston Report).
29. Spear, H. B., 'The British System in Practice', in *The British System*, eds Strang, J. and Gossop, M. (Oxford: Oxford University Press). (In press.)
30. Public Record Office: HO/45/10814/312966.

31. Parsinnen, T. M. (1983) op. cit., p. 176.
32. *Report by the British Government to the League of Nations for 1921 on Opium and other Dangerous Drugs.*
33. *Report by the British Government to the League of Nations for 1924 on Opium and other Dangerous Drugs.*
34. Musto, D. (1991) 'Opium, Cocaine and Marijuana in American History', *Scientific American*, July, pp. 20–7.
35. Rolleston Report, paras 22–4.
36. Parsinnen, T. M. (1983) op. cit., p. 196.
37. Sharpley, A. (1964) *Evening Standard*, 3 and 6 February, 1 May.
38. *Report by the British Government to the League of Nations for 1934 on Opium and Other Drugs.*
39. *Report by the British Government to the United Nations for 1946 on the Traffic in Opium and other Dangerous Drugs.*
40. *Report by the British Government to the League of Nations for 1935 on Opium and Other Drugs.*
41. Spear, H. B. (1969) 'The Growth of Heroin Addiction in the United Kingdom', *British Journal of Addiction*, 64, pp. 1–255.
42. Home Office Drugs Branch Annual Report (1948) Public Record Office: HO 45/24948/651624.
43. *Report to the United Nations by His Majesty's Government of the United Kingdom of Great Britain and Northern Ireland for 1947 on the Traffic in Opium and other Dangerous Drugs.*
44. Frankau, I. M. and Stanwell, P. M. (1960) 'The Treatment of Drug Addiction', *The Lancet*, 24 December, pp. 1377–79.
45. *Report to the United Nations by His Majesty's Government of the United Kingdom of Great Britain and Northern Ireland for 1950 on the Traffic in Opium and other Dangerous Drugs.*
46. Ministry of Health and Department of Health for Scotland (1961) *Drug Addiction. Report of the Interdepartmental Committee* (London: HMSO).
47. Benjamin, I. (1961) Reported in discussion, *British Journal of Addiction*, 57, pp. 92, 93, 102.
48. Frankau, I. M. (1964) 'Treatment in England of Canadian Patients Addicted to Narcotic Drugs', *Canadian Medical Association Journal*, 90, pp. 421–4.
49. Beckett, Dale (1990) Personal communication.
50. Ministry of Health and Scottish Home and Health Department (1965) *Drug Addiction. Second Report of Interdepartmental Committee* (London: HMSO).
51. Home Office (1970) *Dangerous Drugs Statistics 1969*.
52. Parsinnen, T. M. (1983) op. cit., p. 176.
53. Henman, A. (1985) 'Cocaine Futures', in *The Big Deal*, eds Henman, A., Lewis, R. and Malyon T. (London: Pluto Press).
54. Home Office (1984, 1986, 1988) *Tackling Drug Misuse: A summary of the Government's strategy* (London: Home Office).
55. Home Office (1984) *Tackling Drugs Misuse*, para. 4.18.
56. Home Office (1990) *Drugs Prevention Initiative*, pamphlet.
57. Edwards, G. and Strang, J. (1989) 'Cocaine and Crack', *British Medical Journal*, 299, pp. 337–8.

58. *Druglink* (1989) 'Crack Stories from the States', edited extracts of an address by Robert Stutman to the Association of Chief Officers of Police. September/October, pp. 6–7.

59. *Druglink* (1989), op. cit., p. 4.

60. Dorn, N. (1989) *The Times* 26 June.

61. House of Commons (1989) *Crack: The Threat of Hard Drugs in the Next Decade*, Sixth Report of Home Affairs Committee (London: HMSO).

62. Home Office (1991) 'Statistics of the Misuse of Drugs: drug seizures and offenders dealt with, United Kingdom 1990', *Home Office Statistical Bulletin*, issue 19/91.

63. Home Office (1991) 'Statistics of the Misuse of Drugs: Addicts notified to the Home Office, United Kingdom, 1990'. *Home Office Statistical Bulletin*, issue 8/91.

# 3 Cocaine and Crack: The Promotion of an Epidemic
## Philip Bean

Of all the drug scares that have beset the British drug scene over the last 25 years few can compete with the crack–cocaine scare in the late 1980s. Others may have used more shrill language and may have led to more repressive measures, but for sheer hyperbole this scare was the most intense. It lasted about 30 months and ended quietly in August 1990 when the National Task Force, a joint unit of police and customs concerned with controlling crack, whose very name suggested urgency and action, was wound down. During that period, as we were led to believe by some extremists, an epidemic of drug abuse, or rather of crack–cocaine abuse, was due to hit Britain. These fears were based on, or perhaps prompted by a great deal of speculation and much misinformation.

The scare or panic (the terms can be used interchangeably) is defined as existing during a period when acute drug crusades achieve great prominence or legitimacy (Reinarman and Levine, 1981) was largely media-led. It was aided and supported by a small number of self-seeking publicists. They tended to promote their views according to three main assumptions: first, an economic one, whereby it was believed the cocaine barons of South America would seek new markets in Britain, second that America inevitably exports its drug problems, and third, where there is a demand for a drug like cocaine it will be greater where there is an underclass, and a ghettoised black population, who will become instantly addicted to it. (There was, incidentally, little debate on the origin of that underclass but we may leave that aside for the present.)

As with all scares or panics there is of course a point worth making, or at least a point contained deep within the message: in this case that crack use could increase in Britain, and may well still do so in the near future. But scares are not about producing sober statements or providing detached analysis of the current situation. Rather, their supporters try to promote action by arousing fear and moral indignation,

59

usually of a kind which leads to exemplary punishments together with new rules which prohibit behaviour – in this case the aim seemed to be to produce a system not unlike the measures of drug control currently practised in the USA.

## THE MEDIA AND THE DRUG SCARE

It was perhaps fitting that a newspaper, in this case *The Times* (10 August 1990), should officially declare the end of the crack–cocaine panic when it reported the winding up of the National Task Force. In the previous 30 months or so reporting had gone through three distinct phases. In the first phase the scare was created: this phase lasted from about the middle of 1987 to the middle of 1989. The second phase, which lasted for about 12 months, was a period when scepticism began to appear about some of the earlier claims and predictions (though not of course from all newspapers some of whom maintained the same zeal as hitherto) and doubts expressed about the likelihood of an epidemic occurring in Britain. Finally there was the third phase where there was a loss of media interest in the problem. In this phase the media rarely reported crack or cocaine use, indeed they created the impression that the problem no longer existed. This third phase is, however, as important as the others: it should more accurately be seen as a gestation period when a new scare might arise. (And in fact this seemed to be happening in 1991: the new scare surrounded ecstasy MDMA).

In the first phase, media attention varied in terms of the amount and intensity of reporting. Nonetheless the main theme remained consistent: that a crack epidemic would hit Britain in the same way it had hit the United States. There were, however, variations in the type of attention given to these events in the British national press. Not surprisingly, the tabloids personalised the cocaine scare with strong emphasis on identifying individuals and reporting on interviews which featured personalities, or personal violence or sentences from the Courts. In this respect they did not differ from their general approach toward reporting other forms of deviant activity. In contrast the quality papers offered a different fare: they used more 'in-depth analysis' with space being given to the views of experts and policymakers and, where possible, to senior politicians. They too did not differ in their general approach to reporting deviance. The same message was presented: only the style differed. Indeed, how could it be otherwise? The same information was available and the media had to make the best of it; the trick was to give it a slightly different wrapping. Looking back on the period, it seems this particular scare was characterised by the recirculation of limited amounts of information, fed to the media by a small number of self-seeking publicists.

To some extent the British media had to accept what they were given – or rather appeared not to be able to get outside the straitjacket in which they found themselves. There were few experts on hand in Britain and few British research studies upon which to draw. (By the end of 1990 there were only three small British research studies.) Such shortcomings were, however, eagerly filled by a small number of American evangelicals who saw the opportunity to justify American policies. Their message looked no further than a rigid control of supply through law enforcement. To this end the quality papers and the tabloids gave great attention to the crack–cocaine problem as it existed in the USA and, not surprisingly, they reported information given through the eyes of a selected group of American experts – as it so happens mainly employed by the Drugs Enforcement Agency (DEA).

In this first stage fears were aroused and indignation reached its height. This period was later described by *The Times* (10 August 1990) as 'something like panic real or supposed which greeted news of the American crack explosion'. In this, the first phase, crack was described as a 'super drug' which had arrived on the estates in South London and Merseyside (*Observer*, 14 July 1988). Its presence was reported in florid language. 'In 7 short years since it first surfaced in the notorious Los Angeles ghetto of Watts crack has swept through America's cities, snaring hard core drug users, teenagers, businessmen, people from every social station in its wake of psychological dependence and physical craving. It has even killed unborn babies, the innocent victims of crack-addicted mothers' (ibid.). The *Observer* had consistently been the source of some of the most dramatic form of presentation and indeed misinformation, even overtaking some of the tabloids. In a subheading (1 February 1987), crack was described as 'a highly refined and smokeable variant of cocaine, said to be so potent that a single dose can lead to addiction'. Its readers were warned, 'this drug (crack) is a killer. And Britain could be its next target. Its effects on the user are dramatic: within 10 seconds, crack induces an intense euphoria but this rapidly gives way to a craving for more. Without it severe depression and psychological problems follow.' In a final paragraph which is outstanding for producing hints and innuendos but no real facts the *Observer* noted, 'Last November an inquest into the death of a London man was told that he might have died from an overdose of crack. The opening period in a new campaign against drugs has already been fired' (ibid.).

Crack was also presented as a vigorously addictive drug which users would find addictive after two or three contacts (the *Observer* said one). The clearest and most forceful exponent of this message was a DEA agent, Robert Stutman, whose address to the National Drugs Conference of Assistant Chief Police Officers was comprehensively reported. Stutman's information was largely incorrect, his evidence uncorroborated, and his views simpleminded. His style, however, was meat and drink to the British media, as most surely it was intended to be. His influence extended far beyond that specific audience; the Metropolitan Police consulted him in the preparation of their training video on crack/cocaine, and the Home Secretary, who attended the conference said, 'it made a deep impression on me as a Home Secretary' (as Douglas Hurd told the *Daily Mail* on 2 June 1988) and it appears to have made an even deeper impression on the senior policemen there, as well as 'scaring the hell out of the rest of the audience' (ibid.). Douglas Hurd later reported the Stutman speech to the Pompidou group of ministers.

To see some of the impact of this speech consider the following: this gives some of the flavour of Stutman's approach. Stutman said,

> Forget the story that you used to hear that cocaine is not physically addicting, it is physically addicting. They've had to change the definition of addiction in the U.S. to fit cocaine. . . . A study that will be released in the next 2 or 3 weeks will probably say that of all the people who tried crack 3 times or more 75% will become physically addicted at the end of the third time. . . . Right now in the U.S. every major treatment centre will agree . . . crack is considered a virtually incurable addiction. . . . There are no treatment centres that will show any long term remission of any statistically significant number of crack addicts (Stutman, 1989, p. 9 [April]).

*The Sun* picked up the message (25 May 1989): 'Three hits and you can get hooked' and 'Terrifying statistics show that 75% of crack users who are usually between 16 and 35 become hopelessly addicted by inhaling the cocaine derivative *just three times*.' (emphasis original)

This first phase set the scene, as it were. It created levels of anxiety but little in the way of actual information – except, of course, about the position in the USA. The second phase was different: it still portrayed crack as a vigorously addictive and dangerous drug but there was a slight shift in the tone of reporting. The hyperbole was less extreme and a note of scepticism began to appear. For example, when some police officers checked Stutman's claims and tried to find that promised study about '3 hits and you're hooked' it was nowhere to be seen. *The Independent* reported this on 27 July 1989; indeed, this report could be said to be the first indication of a slowdown in the scare tactics used earlier. But by now the fears generated in the first phase of reporting were trickling down to the politicians, to the local media, and even influencing the professional journals. Several British officials, including government politicians as well as local politicians, went to the USA 'to see the crack explosion for real'. Inevitably this meant going to where the action was; this usually involved following American undercover agents on the streets whose task it was to arrange a 'buy and bust' (as was demonstrated to two Home Secretaries, Douglas Hurd and David Waddington). If this was accompanied by gunfire echoing a few blocks from the White House, as indeed it occasionally was, the effects were additionally dramatic. (It has been suggested in some circles that the gunfire was prearranged especially after the visit by Mr David Waddington. This, it appears turned out to be less eventful than hoped for by the American officials as no crack deals were witnessed!)

Two examples will illustrate the point about this 'trickle-down effect' from the mass media to the professional journals. First consider the Home Affairs Committee Report on *Crack* (HMSO, 1989). This produced the same message as was promoted in the media. 'Crack is the most potent and toxic form of cocaine available and is 5 to 10 times as addictive as cocaine taken in other forms. Indeed it can be almost instantly addictive. It can take over a person's life in a week' (ibid., p. viii). Later the report went on to say, 'there is as yet no such person as a fully recovered crack addict. There is no known antidote for crack and no specific treatment for cocaine overdose. The absence of a known cure is one of the most frightening aspects of the cocaine epidemic' (ibid., p. 7).

Second, in an article in *The Magistrate* which must rank as one of the most ill-informed and irresponsible pieces of writing on the subject, the author, a consultant physician at St Lukes Hospital, Bradford said, 'Among all the hard drugs this (crack) will remain at the top as a killer because of its addictive potential. If it is used twice the person is addicted to it. It was highlighted in the press that because of its remarkable addictive properties the drug dealers offer the first dose totally free of cost, and the second dose at half the price; the person is thus addicted to the drug for life' (Mohanty, 1989). Not content with this, the author then added to the fears of those who had to pass sentences on users with the following doubtful and erroneous pieces of information. 'Crack is a new drug with a new delivery system' (it is not a new drug although the delivery system is new) and 'Crack users are former cocaine snorters' (wrong) and 'Crack men have increased sexual activity under the influence of the drug' (wrong again). 'They also exchange sex for drugs contributing to the spread of H.I.V. Because of increased sexual activity women become pregnant. Maternal use of crack is associated with a high rate of miscarriage, premature labour and morbidity and mentality in the infants' (largely incorrect, and no evidence given to support the statements anyway). Given that this type of reporting comes from someone whose status implies some knowledge of the subject, and given that it was aimed at those passing sentence on crack users the damage to the criminal justice system must have been incalculable.

This second phase lasted from about the second half of 1989 to the middle of 1990. It had many features of the first phase: indeed as late as January 1990 *The Times* was still using the same message as before except that the number of 'hits' required for addiction was greater. This, however, was offset by the nature and extent of addiction. Crack was now '10 times more addictive than cocaine' (*The Times*, 7 January 1990). Even so, there was now a slightly more constructive form of national reporting. However, this change at the national level was occasionally offset by new interest from the local media. By now the local media had began to pick up the debate. Some local newspapers had taken it upon themselves to suggest that their local towns or cities should brace themselves for the expected onslaught to come (Nottingham was one. See also Chapter 4 on Glasgow.)

The third phase was different again and reflected a loss of media interest. There was no reduction in crack or cocaine use in Britain generally: all the official indicators such as Customs seizures, prosecutions and data from the Home Office official index suggested the problem was still growing – though not, of course, as fast as was earlier predicted. (See Chapter 1.) This third phase merely represented a period when crack/cocaine use was relegated to secondary levels of media reporting. So, for example, the media would note the official figures of cocaine use but would make little comment – even if use had increased.

These fallow periods in media reporting are as interesting and important as those which are full of media content. They are typical of drug scares and are common features of them. The most notable and influential fallow period in recent times was that of the 1970s. It lasted almost a decade, during which media interest in drugs dropped away – this after an intense period of reporting throughout the 1960s. In the 1980s general interest resumed. It was as if that earlier decade had been a period of rethinking, reformulation and reassessment. The result was a new media stance on drugs and drug addiction, where the activities of users were reported in a less sentimental and less flamboyant form. So too with the crack–cocaine scare of the late 1980s. By 1992 cocaine was rarely considered the demon drug: if anything it was no more serious than any of the others. And by the late part of 1991 was hardly noticed any more.

Fallow periods do not provide opportunities for earlier excesses to be reduced or reported errors to be rectified. All those reports of the dangers of crack, including its addictive potential, remain on file with no attempt by the media to correct mistakes or represent crack–cocaine in a less dramatic form. But how and why fallow periods emerge still remains a mystery.


## ASSUMPTIONS BEHIND THE SCARE

There seems little doubt that the traditional indicators used to detect changes in the extent of drug consumption all pointed to an increase in crack–cocaine use from about 1986 onwards (again, see Chapter 1). Clearly, then, we should not be surprised to see some growth in the use of crack. But the drug scare was more than this: it was about predicting an epidemic, almost a pandemic of global proportions that would hit Britain. Yet on what basis was such a scare promoted? I suggested earlier that the drug scare was fostered on three assumptions. I wish now to look at these to determine to what extent they can be supported.

First, the economic assumption. This was based on a belief that the US market was currently saturated with cocaine. Inevitably then the South American drug barons would seek new markets and, so the argument goes, that would include Britain, along with the continent of Europe. This point of view was put most forcibly by Stutman, but others used it also. Stutman, however, presented it more starkly. He said, 'I will personally guarantee you that 2 years from now (i.e. by

1991) you will have a serious crack problem because. . . . we are so
saturated in the United States with cocaine there ain't enough noses
left to use the cocaine that's coming in. Its got to go somewhere, and
as you know where it's coming is right here (in Britain) (Stutman,
1989, p. 16). A more elegant version appeared in *The Sunday Times*
(15 January 1989). 'The influx of cocaine (into Britain) and the
production of crack is a result of South American cocaine cartels
targeting Europe because they have large surpluses of the drug after
saturating the United States market. Senior Home Office officials say
the cocaine barons are deliberately driving down the price of cocaine
in Europe to create new markets in Britain's depressed inner city
areas' (p. 1).

Yet one wonders why this should be so. Is the US really so
saturated? And if it is, why should the cartels then target Europe
generally, and Britain in particular, to sell their drugs? According to
Harry Shapiro, there are doubts about whether the US market is
indeed saturated (1989), although certain cities and selected areas
may well be. Shapiro argues that New York and Washington, and
perhaps Miami have large crack–cocaine problems. As it happens,
these are also the cities with the highest levels of media attention (and
the highest number of witnesses to Congressional hearings). It is
easy, therefore, to believe that they represent US cities as a whole. In
fact, other cities, including Chicago, have much lower levels, one of
which, Baltimore – lying midway between New York and Washington – has estimated prevalence rates 'in single figures'. Shapiro con-
cludes from the available US evidence that while 'cocaine was the
single most mentioned drug . . . the spread of "reactions" to it is by
no means uniform and it would appear that the major cities in
America vary greatly in the degrees to which they could be said to
have either a cocaine or crack problem' (Shapiro, 1989). Moreover,
even with estimated levels of 25 million US users in 1985 (that is,
lifetime users or those who tried cocaine at least once) and while
current use (defined as use in the past 30 days) rose from 1.6 million
in 1977 to 6 million in 1985 (Kleber, 1988) it is still difficult to know if
this is the upper limit of the US market. Indeed that upper limit for
cocaine was thought to have been reached in 1984 among High
School seniors where it had risen to 5.8 per cent. When crack
appeared in 1984, the numbers began to rise again (ibid., p. 1361).
They could easily rise further. 'Upper limits' are clearly a variable
matter, and may have been reached only in a small number of US
cities. The possibility for greater rates of expansion in others remains.

Yet even if we accept that the US is saturated, Canada with a population of 27 million is clearly not. *The Monthly Digest of Drugs Intelligence Trends* (February 1989) shows some cocaine use in Toronto, but nothing of the order of Detroit, just over the US border. One would have thought drug cartels would have targeted Canada. It would make more economic sense to do so. As Colin Hewitt, Coordinator of UK National Drugs Intelligence Unit, put it in March 1987 when speaking of the UK's position, 'It has long been forgotten by the pessimists that the trail from the coca field to the cocaine dealers here is a long and difficult one and the return journey for the profits is equally hazardous' (Hewitt, 1987, p. 38). The trail to Canada and back is shorter and less hazardous.

No one denies that cocaine is being imported into Britain from South America. The issue is about whether those current imports are precursors of larger amounts due to arrive as a result of a shift in economic attention. If they are, then more is required to sustain this position than a single statement of potential demand. An account of the logistics of developing a new supply system once the cocaine passes through international frontiers is also needed. For example, a rather more complex transportation system would be required to cross the Atlantic than is needed to slip over the Mexican border in a small light aircraft. Those seeing the economic argument solely as a matter of availability and potential supply (that is, in terms of how much can be grown in South America where supplies are plentiful) assume markets are selected on that basis alone. That would seem to be too simple and clearly ignores the nature of such illicit supply systems.

Let us turn now to the second assumption, that America naturally and inevitably exports its drug problems. Does it? (This assumption has another strand which is rarely stated openly but is contained in the debate Stutman uses throughout. He sees American culture as the provider of all new fashions which other countries will automatically follow.) The answer is that it does not. There have been numerous instances where certain types of drug use in America have not been followed in the UK; and, by the same token, where certain forms of drug abuse have occurred in Britain but have not crossed to the US. 'Angel dust', for example, has been much more popular in the US than in Britain, as has 'ice' (d-methamphetamine hydrochloride). Interestingly enough, in the case of 'ice' this seems to have been confined to certain states on the Pacific coast, and Hawaii, without spreading elsewhere (Bean, 1991). In Britain, amphetamines have traditionally retained their popularity without any comparable similar interest in the US. All countries, it seems, have very specific problems which are uniquely theirs.

If the empirical evidence does not support the case, why should the argument have been put in such forceful terms? Or rather, why should the assumptions still be retained? The answer, I think, lies deep within the social milieu in which drugs are taken in the United States, and in the manner in which key personnel see the solution to the problem. By that I mean an orthodox approach in America has now developed which has become a mind set. Alternative policies are not considered, nor is the problem seen to be linked to the structure of American life. It is seen to lie somewhere else, in another country – in this case a country in South America. Occasionally a different approach surfaces – as President Bush seemed to recognise in 1989 – that no solution to the drug menace would be found unless thousands of young Americans could be persuaded that drugs bankrupt, cripple and eventually kill their victim. But in spite of that apparent conversion to a new world-view few policies have emerged to change existing programmes (*The Times*, 19 January 1990). Indeed the new 'drug tsar' William Bennett, whose brief it was to provide the strategy for drug policies in the US in the 1990s has said it was morally plausible to behead drug dealers, and he seriously entertains shooting down planes suspected of carrying drug smugglers. Airborne agents should, he said, have the same enforcement rights as a police officer in the inner city to stop someone speeding away (quoted in Dorn, 1990). Moreover, although the Bennett plan calls for funding and providing treatment programmes, its primary thrust remains on law enforcement with punitive sanctions for drug users. These include revoking driver's licences, sentencing users to 'boot' camps, i.e. prisons offering a 3–6 month military regime, evicting users from public housing, and providing civil commitment proceedings to force drug users into treatment. It also includes such draconian measures as powers to enforce the imposition of sanctions on higher-level education institutes such as universities and colleges. Such institutions then could expect to lose public funds if they are seen to encourage drug use, or rather not actually discourage it among the students (Falco, 1989).

Clearly there has developed an orthodoxy in the USA which cannot believe there are different responses to the drug problem or accept different solutions which do not include American-type law enforcement. Nicholas Dorn reports that disbelievers or sceptics of the orthodox American view are seen in certain American circles as 'not on this planet' (Dorn, 1990). This type of approach, which emphasises reducing supply, also ignores the cultural milieu in which drugs are taken. It sees the problem in terms of pushers and users, and the solution as removing the distributors; first by interdiction at the borders, and then by law enforcement thereafter.

For those seeking to influence UK policy, especially those employed by American law enforcement, the issue becomes more than a debate about an influx of crack–cocaine users. It centres on the promotion of an ideology where the solution involves increasing use of control. That control can be justified in a number of ways as harm done to others or harm done to the user. In the first, crack has been presented as being criminogenic, as promoting and assisting crime. In the second it is presented as being able to induce addiction, or least a form of it; that is, that cocaine addiction is more pervasive than any other form. ('They've had to change the definition of addictio.1 to fit cocaine', said Stutman.)

If we concentrate on the second feature for the moment (for a discussion of the first, see Chapters 4 and 5) it will be of interest to consider a more classical definition of addiction, and link this to the views of some crack users in Britain. (The data is taken from a study conducted in Nottingham in 1989: see Bean, 1990.)

Traditionally 'addiction' has been defined as having mainly physiological effects. It has the following components: first, it produces tolerance; second, there is a tendency to increase the drug up to certain limits, a craving develops, and finally withdrawal is accompanied by physical symptoms. The classic drug of addiction is therefore heroin which has all the features. On this definition crack is not addictive: some of the features of addiction apply; for example, there is some evidence that there is a tendency to increase the dose. On the other hand, there is little evidence to suggest that crack produces tolerance: moreover, it is uncertain if it produces craving, and there is little evidence of physical withdrawal. It may, of course, produce psychological problems, promote a form of habituation or dependency, but those are not features of addiction in the sense in which it is defined above; indeed, some of the crack users in my own study would agree (Bean, 1990). In that study of over 35 users all noted that the effects produced an initial and immediate 'rush' which lasted a matter of minutes followed by a gradual 'come-down' lasting 10–30 minutes. Whereas the 'rush' produced intense pleasure the 'come-down' produced paranoia, irritability, aggression and even violence. ('The down is a bad, bad feeling', said one user.) When asked about tolerance, the results show that only a small number (less than 10 per cent) said they thought a form of tolerance developed – this, however, was difficult to assess because they were unsure of the purity of the drug. Was there a tendency to increase the dose? Again the results are difficult to interpret. Some users thought there was such a tendency but that may be because they liked what they were taking: fatigue said some was the only reason for stopping. When pressed further they said they continued taking the drug because it was enjoyable: they stopped when the money ran out.

When asked about the effects when the drug was not available (i.e. was there a craving and did they experience withdrawal symptoms?) the results are again equivocal. A few users believed a craving developed ('It has a hold, you know' said one) and they thought they could not handle their habit. All said there was a 'come-down' which produced irritability, depression and insomnia in the immediate aftermath and there was common agreement that disturbing psychological reactions developed when the users stopped taking the drug. However, the physical effects on themselves which appear when the drug is withdrawn do not necessarily provide evidence for the existence of withdrawal symptoms. They could be created by the physical changes which are induced by the drug. Most users scoffed at the idea that crack was addictive. 'It's not as dangerous as people make out', said one; 'Three hits and you're hooked – that's crap', said another. Clearly these user responses do not fit the evangelical hype that was promoted by the media or the American orthodoxy. One user aged 32, white, said 'I am a crack user. I have no problem with it. Its great.' He may be the exception or he may be premature in his assessment of the effects, but his description should not be dismissed out of hand anymore than the other extreme view should be accepted unconditionally.

There are, of course, important sociological lessons to be drawn from this. Shifting the definition of addiction to a wider inclusive level involves more than increasing the number of users within its scope – though it certainly does that. Once the definition is allowed to slip its physiological anchor, it allows greater levels of moral evaluations to be included, and hence greater opportunities for controlling such activities as are seen as unworthy or merely disliked. To call an activity 'addictive', as in say gambling, or to call a substance 'addictive' as with crack–cocaine is to justify increasing levels of social control – does not the very term imply a loss of control over one's surroundings? So with crack/cocaine. Claims to see it as an addictive drug can easily be linked to other claims about the need for controls. And with the demand for controls, so there is a corresponding rejection of claims that the user is capable of making choices. Or put another way, other than at the mercy of the supply side of the equation. The circle is complete at least for those wanting greater measures of law enforcement. It remains incomplete if one challenges the wider definitions of addiction or sees drug-taking as more akin to a habit, or simply an attempt to reproduce pleasurable sensations.

The third assumption, that cocaine will flourish wherever there is a ghettorised black population, has two strands to it. The first is that crack–cocaine distribution is controlled in the US partly by the so called 'Yardies' – that is, gangs of Jamaicans. (As Stutman said, they will obviously and inevitably supply the Afro-Caribbean community in Britain.) The second is that crack flourishes in black ghettos; such ghettos are seen to be criminogenic in that crack–cocaine is the favoured drug of the black community. The argument is therefore about ethnicity: blacks or West Indians will supply their own, and crack/cocaine appeals to this type of culture.

The debate about crack use and ethnicity in Britain is likely to continue, for there are some commentators who want to see crack–cocaine as a drug of the black community (again, see Chapter 5). The data obtained so far do not always suggest that the Afro-Caribbean group are dominant in crack use, though they may be over-represented. Again using data in the Nottingham study, it was found that the ethnic composition of this group showed about 40 per cent were Afro-Caribbean, and 60 per cent white Caucasian – none came from other ethnic groups. The social class distribution was linked to ethnicity: black users were more likely to come from class 3, 4 or 5 whereas those coming from social classes 1 and 2 were always white. Those from the upper classes spent the largest amounts, sometimes £1000 to £2000 per week. This data reflects earlier reports on crack or cocaine use in the UK which also links cocaine to middle-class use.

What is missing from the approach that links crack use to ethnicity, especially in the USA, is that it lacks an analysis of the condition of the urban-ghetto social underclass and its rapid degeneration into poverty. It is not simply a truism that young 'crack' dealers have the best-paid job they can get, or are ever likely to get, and, of course, the way they taunt members of the non-drug culture with their new-found wealth is a problem for all. It is, and should be a reasonable question to ask, why crack-dealing is the best job they will ever get. And the obvious answer is that crack-dealers do not live in a world with many opportunities for legitimate income. The massive flow of blue-collar jobs in the late 1960s and 1970s from the large urban areas of American cities coincided with the influx of crack. The exact number of job losses are difficult to calculate, but the estimates are huge. The black ghettos have become vast areas for the unemployed. Small wonder the crack trade is so appealing.

In Britain, according to *The Times*, the position still remains optimistic. 'West Indians in Britain have little in common with blacks in the United States except their colour. Their colour and culture are different, so is their pattern of concentration and their degree of participation in the national economy. The British welfare state offers a more sophisticated system of support to disadvantaged communities than does the American one. . . . Brixton, thank goodness is not South Bronx' (*The Times*, 10 August 1990). This is not to say that there are no ghettoised areas of British cities which resemble their American counterparts where the crack trade is appealing to young black unemployed. But *The Times* believes there are not enough to justify claims that a crack epidemic is due. Unemployment, health care, housing and welfare benefits help keep the problem at bay. We may debate the quality of such services and may find them inadequate, but their existence means the ghettoised underclass of black America is not simply reproduced in British cities.

Such differences in the social milieu cannot easily be ignored. Social problems cannot always be reduced to a matter of moral choice any more than they are explained in terms of cultural determinants. It is no more or less reasonable to assert that people in ghettos take drugs because they are jobless and poor as it is to assert they are jobless and poor because they take drugs. Those in favour of the new orthodoxy are making their own political points. 'The new drug warriors do not see crime plaguing the ghettos for all the reasons it always has but because of the new influence of the chemical "bogeyman". The spread of cocaine and crack is used as an ideological fig leaf to place over unsightly urban ills . . . it is used as a scapegoat on which to blame many economical urban problems . . .' (Reinerman and Levine, 1989).

## WHY THE EPIDEMIC DID NOT HAPPEN

I have suggested that the assumptions on which the drug scene was promoted were basically faulty, and therefore it was not surprising that the crack–cocaine scare did not materialise. But could such an epidemic arise? Perhaps yes, if two features changed. It would be necessary to extend crack–cocaine use beyond the existing using population; and it would be necessary for crack to compete successfully with existing drugs such as amphetamines.

In the first, consider again some of the data from the Nottingham study. In that research it was found that users come from a wide variety of occupations: for the most part employment was and had been erratic (Bean, 1990). Some had been unemployed for a considerable period but a few were in regular employment; one was an accountant, another an office worker and some were self-employed. The data shows crack–cocaine users came from a wider social class distribution than users of most other illicit drugs – with the possible exception of the cannabis user – and particularly those using injectable drugs (Bean and Wilkinson, 1987).

Even so, all the users were poly-users, some, about one-third, had used five or six other drugs during the last year, about one-half had used three or four drugs, again during the last year. Those who had used the most invariably included heroin in their drug history. Their drug-taking profiles usually began with cannabis or amphetamines and ended with crack–cocaine, although crack–cocaine was not a new drug. (The media presented crack as a drug of recent origin but some of these users had taken it five years earlier.) Estimates of the amount spent on crack varied from £30 to £50 per week for the occasional and seemingly controlled user, to £2000 per week for the heavier. Very few gave a clear account of how they financed their crack use, some clearly did so from crime, prostitution being the obvious way, as was drug-dealing. Others, a difficult number to estimate, paid for it out of their legitimate income (Bean, 1990).

These features of the crack population show that crack use has remained within the drug-using population generally. Any epidemic would need to include all that group and others besides. In fact crack use appeared not to go beyond that drug-taking community. One must, of course, be tentative about this, for it could be said that the results obtained in this study were biased by the methodology used – snowballing – for that locks respondents into friendship groups sharing similar lifestyles and produces groups with similar patterns. Also the data obtained from the Nottingham study may not be capable of being generalised to the rest of the UK. Yet the point remains that any epidemic must spread to wider social groups than existing drug users.

The second feature relates to the drug itself and the way it must compete with other drugs in the marketplace if it is to be successful. This, I suggest, was the main reason why a crack epidemic failed to occur, and was more important than any failure of South American cocaine barons to target Britain. The point is that crack must compete with drugs produced through a local industry. That industry is, of course, the amphetamine industry which has a longstanding history of use in most British cities.

Consider first the supply side. Our evidence in the Nottingham study shows that crack which was made locally in Nottingham was supplied by a small number of suppliers (probably four or five who sold the drug as cocaine hydrochloride). They were poly-sellers who supplied a wide range of drugs, including heroin, cannabis and LSD. They came from Birmingham or London so that Nottingham was a satellite to the central supply network. By contrast, amphetamines were locally produced, in large quantities, and were always available. Crack had to compete with this: and in fact failed because the supply of cocaine was more erratic and uncertain. By contrast, amphetamines were supplied regularly. Amphetamine supply had gained a reputation and a foothold and was capable of holding its markets.

On the demand side, crack–cocaine had also to compete with amphetamines in terms of price and effects. In 1991 the price of cocaine was about £80 per gram for which the user got a 20–30 minute high. The price of amphetamines was £12 to £15 per gram, offering a 3–4 hour high. On that basis alone crack must be at a disadvantage and therefore will find it difficult to compete.

Of course, occasional recreational users of cocaine will not be affected by the price of availability of amphetamine, and the middle-class users will not choose amphetamines anyway. But occasional recreation users do not of themselves produce epidemics: for an epidemic to occur, a large number of daily users are needed, able to form the base for the market and act as a platform for an increasing number of recreational users who would in turn quickly become daily users. Nor are there enough middle-class users wanting to take cocaine on a regular basis to make a significant impact on demand. In Nottingham we found two or three such users. If that figure was applied nationally there would still be less than 100 middle-class users spending large sums of money per week: this is hardly likely to create an epidemic.

I am not saying that crack–cocaine is not a problem, nor that it will cease to be a problem; clearly the number of seizures show it to be a widely-used drug. This is, however, different from believing that Britain is to be beset by an epidemic. When we talk of epidemics we need I think to be more concerned with amphetamine use than crack–cocaine.

REFERENCES

Bean, P. T. and Wilkinson C. K. (1987) 'Drug-taking crime and the illicit supply system', *British Journal of Addiction*. Vol. 83, no. 5.
Bean, P. T. (1990) *The Use and Supply of Crack Cocaine*. Report to the Home Office.
—— (1991) '"Ice", poor man's cocaine', *British Medical Journal*, Vol. 303 (20 July), p. 152.
Cotton, P. (1990) 'Medical News and Perspectives'. *Journal of the American Medical Association*, Vol. 263, no. 20, p. 2717.
Dorn, N. (1990) 'This is Britain, buddy', *Druglink*, January/February, p. 11.
Falco, M. (1989) *Winning the Drug War: A national strategy* (Dallas and Hove: Priority Press).
HMSO Home Affairs Committee (1989). *Crack: The threat of hard drugs in the next decade (interim report) Sixth Report*. Session 1988–89 (19 July 1989), no. 536.
Hewitt, C. (1987) Report to the UK National Drugs Intelligence Unit (mimeo).
Kleber, H. D. (1988) 'Epidemics of cocaine abuse: America's present, Britain's future', *British Journal of Addiction*, Vol. 83, pp. 1359–71.
Mohanty, K. C. (1989) 'Crack', *The Magistrate*, Vol. 45, no. 11, pp. 190–1.
Newcombe, R. and Matthews, L. (1989) 'Crack in Liverpool', *Druglink*, September/October, p. 16.
Reinerman, C. and Levine, H. G. (1989) 'The crack attack: politics and media in America's latest drug scare', in Best, J. (ed.), *Images of Issues* (Aldine Press), pp. 115–37.
Shapiro, H. (1989) 'Crack – the story so far', *Health Education Journal*, Vol. 48, no. 3, pp. 140–4.
Stutman, R. M. (1989) 'Crack, its effects on a city and a law enforcement response', Papers given to the 9th Annual National Drugs Conference of Assistant Chief Police Officers, Wales (mimeo).
Tippell, S. (1989) 'Crack in London', *Druglink*, September/October, p. 12.
Trebach, A. (1982) *The Heroin Solution* (New Haven: Yale University Press).
Wilson, J. Q. (1990) 'Drugs and crime', in Tonry, M. and Wilson, J. Q. (eds), *Drugs and Crime* (Chicago: University of Chicago Press).

# 4 'A Very Greedy Sort of Drug': Portraits of Scottish Cocaine Users

## The Scottish Cocaine Research Group*

Yeah . . . in the first year, I only did it twice, then the year after, went mad for it: every night for three months. I spent about a grand [£1000] a week, ludicrous when you think about it. Every night until about 6 in the morning. I even used to go out and score at 2 in the morning . . . and that would be the third time that night. That's the way cocaine gets you. That's why it's a complete waste of time. . . .

(40-year-old Scottish male intensive cocaine user)

### WHY STUDY COCAINE IN SCOTLAND?

In Scotland, official evidence of cocaine use is patchy, although an average of 26 persons per year were successfully prosecuted for cocaine offences during the whole of the 1980s. Scotland has about 10 per cent of the British population, but has not yet matched even that level in numbers or volumes of cocaine seizures, or in persons dealt

* Current SCRG members include: Jason Ditton, Kathryn Farrow, Alasdair Forsyth, Richard Hammersley, Gillian Hunter, Tara Lavelle, Ken Mullen and Ian Smith (University of Glasgow); John Davies and Marion Henderson (University of Strathcyde) Valerie Morrison (University of Edinburgh); and David Bain (Castlemilk Drug Project, Glasgow); Lawrence Elliot (HIV and AIDS Resource Centre, Ruchill Hospital, Glasgow); Andy Fox (The Bridge Project, Ayr); Brian Geddes (Aberdeen Drugs Action); Ronnie Green (Easterhouse Committee on Drug Abuse, Glasgow); John Taylor (Southern General Hospital, Glasgow) and Philip Dalgarno, Ian Ferguson, Sam Phillips and Stephen Watt. Correspondence about this chapter to: Jason Ditton, Criminology Research Unit, 61 Southpark Avenue, Glasgow University, GLASGOW, G12 8LF.

*Table* 4.1   Official data on cocaine in Scotland

|  | 1980 | 1981 | 1982 | 1983 | 1984 | 1985 | 1986 | 1987 | 1988 | 1989 |
|---|---|---|---|---|---|---|---|---|---|---|
| *Number of seizures*[1] | | | | | | | | | | |
| Scotland | 15 | 28 | 20 | 45 | 58 | 41 | 36 | 42 | 28 | 34 |
| All UK | 445 | 503 | 389 | 684 | 889 | 662 | 635 | 717 | 829 | 2045 |
| Scotland as % of UK | 3 | 6 | 5 | 7 | 7 | 6 | 6 | 6 | 3 | 2 |
| *Volume of seizures (kg)*[1] | | | | | | | | | | |
| Scotland | – | – | 0.2 | 0.1 | 0.5 | 0.4 | 0.1 | 0.1 | 29.8 | 0.1 |
| All UK | 40 | 21 | 19 | 80 | 65 | 85 | 103 | 407 | 323 | 499 |
| Scotland as % of UK | – | – | 1 | (*) | 1 | (*) | (*) | (*) | 9 | (*) |
| *Persons found guilty, cautioned, or dealt with by compounding*[1] | | | | | | | | | | |
| Scotland | 15 | 27 | 26 | 30 | 39 | 29 | 20 | 26 | 26 | 22 |
| All UK | 476 | 566 | 426 | 563 | 698 | 632 | 449 | 518 | 591 | 786 |
| Scotland as % of UK | 3 | 5 | 6 | 5 | 6 | 5 | 5 | 5 | 4 | 3 |
| *New cocaine addicts notified to the Home Office*[2] | | | | | | | | | | |
| Scotland | 6 | 6 | 10 | 10 | 30 | 69 | 35 | 16 | 9 | 14 |
| All UK | 147 | 174 | 214 | 345 | 471 | 490 | 520 | 431 | 462 | 527 |
| Scotland as % of UK | 4 | 4 | 5 | 3 | 6 | 14 | 7 | 4 | 2 | 3 |

*Notes*
* More than zero, but less than 1%.
1. Source, Scotland data, Table 3.12, *Statistics of the Misuse of Drugs: Seizures and Offenders Dealt with, United Kingdom, 1989 (Scotland Tables)*, Home Office. Source, UK Data: Table 1.1, *Statistics of the Misuse of Drugs: Seizures and Offenders Dealt with, United Kingdom, 1989*, Home Office Statistical Bulletin, 24/90, September, 1990.
2. Source, Scotland Data: Table 2, *Statistics of the Misuse of Drugs: Addicts Notified to the Home Office, United Kingdom, 1989 (Scotland Tables)*, Home Office. Source, UK Data: Table 2, *Statistics of the Misuse of Drugs: Addicts Notified to the Home Office, United Kingdom, 1989*, Home Office.

with in court or notified to the Home Office as cocaine 'addicts' (see Table 4.1).

Of the few court cases in Scotland in which there were contested trials and for other reasons were apparently newsworthy, Glasgow's 'happy dust gang' received the most coverage. The 'gang' – in reality, a small group of local businessmen (one owned a travel agency, one a bakery, another was a disc jockey on a local radio station) were caught by police in the early 1980s 'after hearing that huge amounts of cocaine were circulating among Glasgow's trendy set' (*Scotsman*, 13 October 1989).

As for professional evidence, one substantial survey reported over three times as much cocaine use as opiate use among young Scottish populations (Plant, Peck and Samuel, 1985), and more recent work has shown that cocaine is at least used as an occasional luxury drug by some illicit drug users, especially those who are heavier poly-drug users (Hammersley, Lavelle and Forsyth, 1990; Hammersley *et al.*, 1989; Morrison and Plant, 1990).

Of course, all the newspapers (apart from the *Evening Standard*) carrying the cocaine and crack–cocaine stories emanating from Fleet Street are widely available in Scotland, and we can expect (indeed, we will later see) Scottish cocaine users to be influenced by them, and in particular by the media panic on crack–cocaine of the summer of 1989 (Hammersley *et al.*, 1990). Scotland itself has had a pretty lean time in the mythological stakes, although not for want of trying:

COCAINE CAPITAL'S EVIL TRADE GROWS. Cocaine from South America is flooding into Edinburgh on a scale never seen before. . . .
(*Glasgow Daily Record*, 3 February 1986).

This report was sensibly denied by a colleague of the person the remarks were attributed to with the disclaimer, 'the suggestion that there is more cocaine in Edinburgh than there used to be is true – but you could say that about anywhere'. Seven months later, a Scottish Sunday paper had another go:

NOW CRACK SPREADS TO SCOTLAND
(*The Sunday Post, 21 September 1986*)

No evidence yet again, and the same expert was quoted as saying, wearily, 'crack is just another form of cocaine, and cocaine is already used in Edinburgh by many people, it could be some people in Edinburgh are already experimenting with it'. Scotland had to wait nearly 3 years for the next panic headline:

WARNING ON 'CRACK' REACHING SCOTLAND
(*Glasgow Herald*, 30 June 1989)

Things seemed to be looking up, but the first sentence opened with the words, 'The cocaine derivative "crack" has not yet found its way into Scotland . . .'. Undaunted, and heady with expectation, the run-up for the new year witnessed the following headline:

COPS WAIT AS DRUG EVIL CREEPS NORTH
(*Glasgow Daily Record*, 26 December 1989)

The opening paragraph continued, 'Scots detectives are bracing themselves for the first appearance of the dreaded drug crack north of the border. They believe 1990 will see the first seizure of the drug, probably in Ediburgh or Glasgow. So far there have been only rumours that the cocaine-based drug is here. But police in Scotland had made NO seizures."

Although there was no evidence of the use of crack-cocaine, recipes for making it from cocaine quietly appeared in a small circulation give-away magazine until the local press got hold of the story:

DEADLY DRUG RECIPE SHOCK
(*Glasgow Evening Times*, 8 February 1987)

There is now undeniable evidence pointing to the fact that Scotland is used as, at least, a major cocaine transhipment locale. In 1988 the then largest UK seizure of cocaine (of 28 kg, allegedly worth £3 million) took place in Greenock. On 10 January 1991, 500 kg of cocaine (allegedly worth £50 million) was seized near Inverness. This is currently the largest single UK seizure. Most recently, a further 30 kg (allegedly worth £4.5 million) was discovered in the propeller shaft of a ship docked at Hunterston, Ayrshire on 23 May 1991.

If cocaine is not being used in quantity by Scottish delinquents, and there is some evidence (from police seizures) of the availability of cocaine in wholesale quantities in Scotland, then who, if anybody, is using it?

Secondly, what effects does cocaine have? Crucially, does use of cocaine foster 'addiction'? It is clear that, at least in America, cocaine use can lead to dependence although the proportion of cocaine users who become dependent may be quite low. In 1985 the prevalence of cocaine use among American high-school seniors was 17 per cent (Johnston *et al.*, 1986). The proportion of cocaine-dependent Americans currently in their early twenties is considerably less. The marketing, method of ingestion and metabolism of crack–cocaine may nonetheless have raised the incidence of cocaine-dependence (Kleber, 1989).

In contrast, in Amsterdam, where cocaine is usually snorted, Cohen (1989, pp. 13–14) concluded:

Support for the hypothesis that the pharmacological characteristics of cocaine make problematic (high) use patterns inevitable was not found. On the contrary, there are no indications that our group of experienced cocaine users lost control and developed into compulsive high level users.

In the light of the even-then looming media crack–cocaine panic, the Scottish Cocaine Research Group was established in March 1989 to see whether Scottish cocaine users existed, and, if so, whether they resemble American crack smokers or Amsterdam cocaine snorters. It was decided to adopt the 'snowball' method of contacting respondents (Biernacki and Waldorf, 1981), which has been used in America, Canada, Amsterdam and Australia (respectively Chitwood and Morningstar, 1985; Erickson, Adalf and Petrie, 1987; Cohen, 1989; and Mugford and Cohen, 1989; respectively), and to use a modified and translated version of Cohen's (1989) questionnaire.

Seventeen members of the SCRG interviewed cocaine-using subjects known to them or suggested by other interviewees. These interviews were conducted in Glasgow, Edinburgh, Dundee, Aberdeen, Ayr and at other Scottish locations. All were completed between the beginning of July 1989 and the end of July 1990.

To qualify as a cocaine user and thus for inclusion in this study group, Scottish users had to have used cocaine at least once in the past three years. Users had to be interviewed in Scotland, but needn't be Scottish (i.e. by any parental or residential nationality criteria). To qualify, the minimum one use in the previous three years needn't have been in Scotland, but if it wasn't, then the user must have used at least once in Scotland prior to that. Of the 92, 24 per cent (n = 22) had used cocaine between 1 and 5 times in the previous 3 years, 23 per cent (n = 21) between 6 and 10 times, 26 per cent (n = 24) between 11 and 30 times, 16 per cent (n = 15) between 31 and 99 times, and 11 per cent (n = 10) over 100 times.

THE STUDY GROUP

The study group was 74 per cent male (n = 68), and 26 per cent female (n = 24). Less than a fifth (17 per cent) were aged 25 and under, nearly a third (29 per cent) were aged 26–30, a fifth (20 per cent) aged 31–35, another fifth (23 per cent) aged 36–40, and a few (10 per cent) aged 41 or over. The mean age of the group was just over 22 years old.

Just over a quarter (26 per cent) were unattached, 22 per cent had a steady partner of less than a year, and 52 per cent had a steady partner of a year or more. Slightly over a quarter (26 per cent) lived with their partner (a further 23 per cent with a partner and children), and only 15 per cent lived alone.

Thus far, this could be a description of all or any of the 'new' drug users of the 1980s (Pearson, 1987). A model – working-class injectors using ever-increasing amounts of drugs and living in council houses and from a mixture of state benefits and the profits from property crimes or prostitution – that was as difficult to establish when it was first suggested (Ditton and Speirits, 1981) as it is hard to disestablish today. From here on, this group of cocaine users seems quite different.

To start with, although a minority (10 per cent) had no educational qualifications, about a third (29 per cent) had some school qualifications, more (41 per cent) had college or university qualifications and the remaining 20 per cent had professional qualifications or higher degrees.

Total incomes were also uneven, with 4 per cent having gross annual incomes of over £25 000, 7 per cent having incomes of between £15 000, and £25 000 a year, 38 per cent incomes between £10 000 and £15 000, 24 per cent with incomes between £6000 and £10 000, 13 per cent between £4000 and £6000, 7 per cent incomes of between £2000 and £4000, and the remaining 7 per cent with incomes below £2000.

The fact that most of these cocaine users were employed distinguishes them even more markedly from the 'new' stereotype of the British drug user. The additional fact that a greater proportion of the cocaine users are in higher-status occupations is quite startling. As Table 4.2 shows, nearly twice as many cocaine users have 'professional' and 'middle' status occupations as is true for the employed Scottish population.

Perhaps surprisingly, none of these sociodemographic variables was related to any measure of subjects' past or recent cocaine use, although within the sociodemographic variable set, relationships were in the expected direction.

Twenty of the 92 had received some medical or other treatment in the preceeding three years because of their use of drugs (only four because of their use of cocaine), and 10 had received a criminal conviction in the same period for some offence related to their drug use (only one because of cocaine use). In all, five had received treatment and convictions, 15 had only been treated and 9 only

*Table* 4.2   Usual occupation of cocaine users and general Scottish population

| Occupational status | N = 85 n | (%) | (%) | 255 996 n |
|---|---|---|---|---|
| *Professional* | 33 | (39) | (20) | 51 393 |
| 1 Professional and related supporting management senior national and local government managers | 13 | (15) | (3) | 6 538 |
| 2 Professional and related in education, welfare and health | 18 | (21) | (14) | 36 197 |
| 3 Professional and related in science, engineering, technology and similar fields | 2 | (2) | (3) | 8 658 |
| *Middle* | 31 | (37) | (21) | 53 351 |
| 4 Literary, artistic and sports | 24 | (28) | (1) | 1 461 |
| 5 Managerial | 6 | (7) | (7) | 18 394 |
| 6 Clerical and related | 1 | (1) | (13) | 33 496 |
| *Working* | 21 | (25) | (59) | 151 252 |
| 7 Selling | – | (–) | (6) | 14 913 |
| 8 Security and protective service | – | (–) | (3) | 5 762 |
| 9 Catering, cleaning, hairdressing and other personal services | 8 | (9) | (11) | 27 113 |
| 10 Farming, fishing and related | 1 | (1) | (2) | 5 534 |
| 11 Materials processing; making and repairing excluding metal and electrical | – | (–) | (7) | 18 236 |
| 12 Processing, making, repairing and related (metal and electrical) | 7 | (8) | (11) | 27 149 |
| 13 Painting, repetitive assembling, product inspecting, packaging and related | 1 | (1) | (3) | 8 681 |
| 14 Construction, mining and related (not identified elsewhere) | 1 | (1) | (4) | 9 926 |
| 15 Transport operating, materials moving and storing and related | 2 | (2) | (7) | 16 895 |
| 16 Miscellaneous | – | (–) | (3) | 6 272 |
| 17 Inadequately described and not stated (includes criminal occupations) | 1 | (1) | (4) | 10 771 |

*Notes*
Cocaine user total excludes 7 'Others, not applicable'.
Scottish population data extracted from Tables 1 and 3 of the Registrar General for Scotland's *Census 1981, Economic Activity* (Edinburgh: HMSO, 1984). The raw data reflect a 10 per cent sample of the working population.

convicted. Thus, 63 (69 per cent) were, in these two senses, officially 'invisible', and only five in both senses, fully 'visible'. Like Cohen (1989, p. 28), we had sought 'invisible' users but not rejected interviews with those with a history of treatment or convictions. So, we have not weeded out the 'visibles' because of this, and also because their number was too small to influence significantly the results.

*Table* 4.3   Location of first use of cocaine (percentages)

|  | N = 92 |
| --- | --- |
| Glasgow | 25 |
| Edinburgh | 22 |
| Other Scotland | 13 |
| Other Britain | 25 |
| Abroad | 15 |

*Note*   All percentages are rounded.

## THE FIRST TIME THEY USED COCAINE

Most of the 'new' drug users of the 1980s began using opiates in their teens or early twenties. Not so for this group of cocaine users. Although 30 per cent first used cocaine before they were 20 years old and a further 48 per cent before they were 25, another 14 per cent didn't first use cocaine until they were in their late 20s, and 7 per cent not until they were in their early thirties.

Even more noticeably, this first cocaine use was, for 2 per cent, as long ago as the 1960s. A further 17 per cent didn't start until the early 1970s, with another 22 per cent using cocaine for the first time in the late 1970s. Only 61 per cent of this group first used cocaine in the 1980s (27 per cent between 1980 and 1984, and the remainder since then).

Although all members of the study group had used cocaine in Scotland at least once, a substantial minority had first tried it elsewhere. Location of first use is shown in Table 4.3

It has been known for some time that more than 10 per cent of cocaine consumed illegally is transhipped on commercial aircraft (US Department of State, 1984). Several Scottish respondents mentioned having been first introduced to cocaine actually in America, and this is perhaps the first indication that the same jets may well be ferrying consumers to the cocaine, as well as cocaine to the consumers. This man, a 29-year-old male casual user, was fairly typical:

Well, I was visiting my cousin in America, and there it was! On the grocery list on the side of the fridge: 'POT'! When I turned up, one of the first things he added to it was 'CHARLIE' [cocaine]. I didn't know what it meant until the weekend. . . .

In another sense, too, his experience, was typical: he first consumed cocaine, as did 46 per cent of this study group, at home (32 per cent in a friend's house, and 14 per cent in their own house). A further 27 per cent first tried cocaine at a party, 17 per cent first at work, university/college or elsewhere, and 10 per cent at a club, bar, restaurant or disco.

The vast majority (95 per cent) first used cocaine intranasally ('snorting'), with only 2 per cent injecting, 2 per cent swallowing and 1 per cent smoking. Most (80 per cent) were given the cocaine free the first time they tried it (only 11 per cent asked for it), but a surprisingly high 20 per cent bought it for themselves the first time. This man's experience is fairly typical (he is a 49-year-old male casual user), and he shows, again, that Scotland's distance from South American sources doesn't necessarily mean that retail cocaine is heavily adulterated:

> several years ago, a friend of mine called to see me. He'd just come back from Lima, and he'd got some utterly pure coke. I must say I was impressed. Quite apart from the fact that it almost took my head off, it was quite unlike anything I've had since the 1960s. The quality seems to be a real problem nowadays.

COCAINE CAREERS

All the Scottish cocaine users were asked detailed questions about the frequency, route and quantity of their cocaine use during three periods: during their first year of use, during their 'heaviest period' of use, and during the three months prior to the interview. A summary of replies is shown in Table 4.4.

Interviewers initially approached the 'heaviest period' section of the questionnaire with some trepidation as their lack of experience with cocaine research offered no confidence that users would know what was meant. Further, most members of the SCRG were experienced in dealing with 'new' opiate-type drug users whose pattern of use was overwhelmingly one of almost endless escalation of dose and frequency.

However, with cocaine users, even those interviewees whose own use career featured no 'heaviest period', understood well what the term meant (probably from observation of the use patterns of other users). For those who did recall a 'heaviest period', this began on

*Table* 4.4   Subsequent use of cocaine (during three irregular periods)

| | first year % | N = 92 heaviest period % | last 3 months % |
|---|---|---|---|
| *Frequency* weekly or more | 30 | 62 | 9 |
| *Route* Injecting | 5 | 8 | 2 |
| *Amount* 100mg or more | 32 | 49 | 17 |

*Note*   All percentages are rounded.

average 2½ years after first use of cocaine, and lasted, again on average, just over ten months. The user quoted at the beginning of this chapter typifies the 78 per cent of this group who did have a 'heaviest period', but these two users are more typical of the 22 per cent who didn't:

> I don't think I had a "heaviest period" – I just used the same amount slightly more often.
>
> (21-year-old female casual user)

> I never really had a heavy period, although I've occasionally gone through a gram on my own.
>
> (29-year-old male casual user)

Most respondents' cocaine use in their first year of use was sporadic, as these interviewees testify:

> Sometimes I'd do quite a lot in a month, and then none for ages.
>
> (30-year-old male casual user)

> If there was quite a lot available, and if I'd spare cash then I'd buy some. If I'd no money or whatever, I can't say I was ever particularly upset [if I couldn't get any].
>
> (27-year-old male casual user)

In general, in the first year of use, amounts of cocaine used (users were asked how much cocaine they used in a day when they used cocaine) were greater than in the three months prior to interview, but less than during their 'heaviest period' of use. By far the greatest

majority snorted during all three periods, and these three responses
were typical:

> Snorting is seen as more glamorous.
>                              (27-year-old male casual user)

> I tried swallowing it a few times, but I didn't get the same high
> effect. It was much slower, and didn't last as long.
>                              (27-year-old male regular user)

> I was scared to do it any other way than snorting. I think I had an
> idea that I'd get addicted, especially if I injected.
>                              (30-year-old female ceased user)

Those who used other methods suggested that circumstances forced
the choice:

> This depended on the situation. If it wasn't cool to snort in a club,
> I'd swallow it rolled up in a cigarette paper.
>                              (30-year-old male casual user)

Only a handful injected, more during their 'heaviest period' of use
(when a further 4 per cent usually freebased when they used), and
fewer during the three months prior to interview. As one 32-year-old
male casual user put it:

> I wouldn't use any intraveneously now at all. I haven't done for a
> long time: it's too dangerous and too obvious.

Most of those who are still using cocaine seem relaxed about their
use, as these two respondents illustrate:

> If I go for a bit, I do it in a oner [all at once] . . . then I don't do it
> for months.
>                              (29-year-old male casual user)

> The amount I use depends on whether I'm working or just . . . you
> know, social life . . . I'd use more before going on stage.
>                              (26-year-old female regular user)

Some users had deliberately reduced their cocaine intake:

> It's purely recreational these days, so I'd do it more or less as the
> situation arose.
>                              (30-year-old male casual user)

> I can only afford to do coke when I'm out on a tour [as part of a
> roadie team for a rock band]. When I'm at home, I can't afford it,

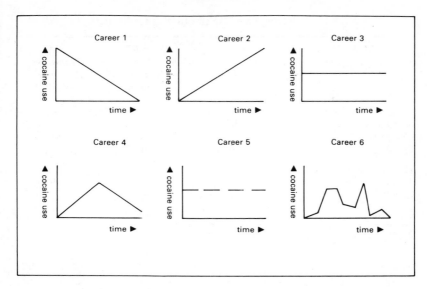

*Figure* 4.1   Cocaine careers

and I lose touch with the people I get it from.

(21-year-old female casual user)

Altogether some twelve users had stopped using cocaine altogether when interviewed. These two offered reasons:

Then I got a bit bored with it, I also got promoted and then married, so it had to stop.

(38-year-old male ceased user)

Since the children appeared on the scene, I've stopped taking almost everything except cannabis. An overwhelming sense of parental responsibility, I suppose.

(39-year-old female ceased user)

Finally, all those interviewed were shown the six graphs of cocaine 'careers' reproduced in Figure 4.1, and asked which came nearest to representing their cocaine use over time. Most respondents spent a great deal of time getting this right (particularly those who opted instead to complete a blank graph which was provided as an alternative), especially the one blind respondent, who first of all had to master the concept of graphical representation.

Interestingly, given the force of the 'new' stereotype of the ever-

*Table* 4.5   Use of other drugs

| | Used ever % | N = 92 Used last 3 months % | Would use if offered free % |
|---|---|---|---|
| Amphetamines | 97 | 49 | 62 |
| Cannabis | 99 | 90 | 90 |
| Opiates | 70 | 14 | 39 |
| Hallucinogens | 90 | 46 | 55 |
| Tranquillisers | 59 | 14 | 14 |
| Crack | 8 | – | 38 |
| Cocaine | 100 | 87 | 90 |

*Note*   All percentages are rounded.

escalating dose, none of the 92 cocaine users chose career 2 (slowly more). Some 17 per cent chose career 1, 16 per cent career 3, 25 per cent career 4, 18 per cent career 5 and 24 per cent career 6. However, absence of any evidence of addiction in this sense and for this unrepresentative and rather middle-class group does not mean that addiction in other senses is not present (craving, loss of tolerance, depression on cessation) for members of this group, or that addiction in the sense of an ever-escalating dose (i.e. career 2) might not be present with far greater frequency with other types of cocaine user.

USING OTHER DRUGS

All respondents were asked whether or not they had ever used 'amphetamines, cannabis (marijuana, hash), opiates (opium, heroin, morphine), hallucinogens (LSD, magic mushrooms), tranquillisers, and crack', whether they had used them in the last three months, and whether or not they would use them if they were offered them free. Results are given in Table 4.5.

It is perhaps surprising, in a group of employees most of whom have remained invisible to both drug enforcement and drug service delivery, to find such a broad history of illicit poly-drug use – and such a preparedness to continue illegal drug use in the future.

Amphetamine (often dubbed the 'poor man's cocaine') use isn't surprising. As two Scottish respondents noted,

I only use amphetamine because of shortage of cocaine, or because of poor quality cocaine.

(30-year-old male regular user)

The difference between speed and coke is the difference between wine and champagne.

(24-year-old female casual user)

Cannabis is so widely available that it is merely surprising that only 90 per cent had used it in the three months prior to interview. Lifetime prevalence (but not last three months) of opiates is high, yet several respondents only answered 'yes' to that question because it included 'opium' as an example. One 39-year-old male casual user spoke for many:

It's 'yes', but only because I used to smoke opium occasionally. I wouldn't touch heroin or morphine.

Use of hallucinogens is high (Scotland has a climate which is kind to mushrooms), and tranquillisers low. The answers to questions on crack–cocaine are intriguing. All respondents were interviewed after the crack–cocaine media panic of the summer of 1989, and whereas only 8 per cent had ever used crack–cocaine (none in the prior three months) 38 per cent claimed they would use crack–cocaine if offered it free, and this included 5 of the 7 who had tried it.

These two interviewees hadn't yet tried crack–cocaine but were game for (almost) anything:

You can get anything where I come from. I know it's illegal and also against work rules, but you can usually get whatever you want. When I get the chance I'll try crack and anything I haven't tried already.

(30-year-old male user)

Crack? Yes, I'll try anything as long as it wasn't smack. As you get older, you move on. It has more to do with who you are with and what the group is into.

(27-year-old female casual user)

Yet the following two interviewees were typical of the 62 per cent who wouldn't try crack–cocaine if offered it free:

Never! It really frightens me! It's well-named. A lot of people will crack under it.

(29-year-old male casual user)

No way! What I read about crack scares me. I know it's hype but it still scares me.

(25-year-old female casual user)


EFFECTS OF COCAINE

Respondents were given a long and evenly-mixed list of possible advantages and disadvantages of cocaine use. Looking first at the advantages, nearly all (96 per cent) agreed that cocaine use 'makes you high, relaxed' and that it 'increases feelings of excitement'. Only slightly fewer (94 per cent) agreed that cocaine use 'makes you feel more energetic', with one 27-year-old male casual user adding:

The main reason I use it is for energy and to have fun after long hours at work.

Another (perhaps feeling his age) added:

I take coke for a big 'up' . . . to keep you going all night.

(40-year-old male casual user)

Some 85 per cent and 75 per cent felt that cocaine use 'increases your self-confidence' and 'makes you communicate better' respectively. Several chose to make comments relating to cocaine use in these senses. First, on the effect with acquaintances:

You're outgoing, no shyness, you talk to anybody.

(25-year-old female casual user)

I've gained a couple of friends through having a couple of toots [of cocaine] with them.

(29-year-old male casual user)

I can relate and get on with people I've never met before . . . I'm totally at ease.

(28-year-old male casual user)

I find it easier to get to know complete strangers at parties. If they're hostile, I tend not to be, and this breaks down barriers.

(32-year-old male casual user)

It's a very sociable drug. I can take it when other people haven't and not make them feel ill at ease.

(27-year-old female ceased user)

Second, on the effect with intimates (or intended intimates):

> I become very affectionate towards my girlfriend, and we usually iron out any domestic problems we may have.
>
> (30-year-old male ceased user)

> I used to take it and go out and chase women. I always seemed to have more success with my chat-up lines.
>
> (38-year-old male ceased user)

Some 75 per cent also agreed that cocaine use 'prolongs sex and makes it more pleasurable', with 69 per cent agreeing that it 'makes you more creative'. One 30-year-old female ceased user added:

> I think this is more true of cocaine than of any other drug. As an artist, I feel it gives me an ability and insight that I wouldn't get with, say, acid [LSD].

Interspersed with these seven possible advantages was a set of seven possible disadvantages. More users (75 per cent) agreed that cocaine use 'is too expensive' than any other suggested disadvantage. Many also chose to comment:

> No doubt I'd have done more coke, and probably a lot less of the more harmful drugs if it had been a more realistic price.
>
> (30-year-old male casual user)

> [Expense is] one of the main reasons I don't use it any more.
>
> (36-year-old male casual user)

> I suppose so. I don't really buy enough to really notice. I think that Ecstasy or even dope (marijuana) is a lot more expensive . . . for what you get.
>
> (24-year-old female casual user)

> Most good Class A drugs are [expensive], though: look at Ecstasy.
>
> (28-year-old male casual user)

As a subsidiary question put at the end of interviews with users who were prepared to give up even more time, each was asked how much cocaine they would have used if it had been half the price. Feelings were mixed:

> I don't know that I'd use any more of it if it was cheaper.
>
> (22-year-old male regular user)

To be truthful, if it was half the price, I'd probably do twice as much.

(29-year-old male casual user)

I'd have used more if it had been half the price, but then I'd have drunk more alcohol had it been half the price, eaten more food had it been half price.

(32-year-old male regular user)

A further 57 per cent agreed that cocaine use 'leads to sleeplessness, insomnia' (some, of course, desired this; such as the 40-year-old male quoted earlier, who claimed he took 'coke for a big 'up' . . . to keep you going all night'). And although only 32 per cent agreed that cocaine 'creates psychological dependence', many chose to comment on the issue. First, some who used food as a comparison:

Cocaine can be addictive, as can be ice-cream, or anything you like. It's not addictive like smack is addictive.

(36-year-old male casual user)

I don't think I ever got into it enough to find out. It could be. Then again, I'm 'psychologically dependent' on cheese and onion crisps.!

(30-year-old male casual user)

Now, some who had experience with nicotine:

Maybe . . . I had a wee bit of trouble when I cut it down, but like you say, it was all in my head. Still, [stopping was] easier than stopping smoking [tobacco] . . .

(25-year-old male casual user)

I can take it or not. Cigarettes are worse . . .

(22-year-old male regular user)

A couple more specified the limits in legal terms:

Tricky one . . . used to piss me off if we didn't have any in the house, but it's not like smack or something . . . where you'd rob someone for money to buy some, so probably not.

(32-year-old male regular user)

Not for me . . . I wouldn't mug old ladies to get some money to score coke.

(30-year-old male casual user)

Finally, two were less than completely sure:

I don't think so. At least I can take it or leave it without any bother.

(28-year-old male casual user)

Maybe so, but I've never really been affected by it. I've heard that some people do get mentally hooked.

(30-year-old female ceased user)

Thirty per cent agreed that cocaine 'has unpleasant side effects' (one 41-year-old female ceased user put it pithily: 'headache in the morning, and emotionally disturbed 24 hours later . . .'), nearly as many (29 per cent) that cocaine 'makes you aggressive, irritated', and 25 per cent that it 'makes you feel depressed'.

Some 13 per cent claimed that cocaine use 'reduces sexual performance', and 9 of the 12 who claimed this had also claimed that cocaine use 'prolongs sex and makes it more pleasurable'. This isn't necessarily a contradiction, but clearly more research is needed in this area.

Users were encouraged to list any additional positive or negative effects, and, perhaps surprisingly given the determination of most to use cocaine again if offered free, tended to list more bad than good effects. Being able to drink more alcohol ('but with less effect') was cited more than once, and by men as well as women. Unwanted sensitivity to sunlight, 'very bad shakes in the mornings, and have trouble doing simple things like cleaning my teeth', proneness 'to colds in the summer', 'anxiety attacks when out in crowded streets', 'total memory lapses', 'feelings of intellectual inadequacy when the after effect has worn off', 'extreme nervousness sometimes. The feeling of not wanting to leave the house', losing 'my sense of balance', are just some of the consequences mentioned. One man had a particularly memorable experience:

> Once, I was in a house, and there was 2 ounces [of cocaine] being cut up, and I didn't even know it was going on. But I helped, doing the weighing, and I was making up parcels all night . . . until 7 in the morning. I went to go out for coffee, but I couldn't walk as I'd done [taken] so much [cocaine], and I ended up spending 7 days in hospital, although I never told them what I'd been doing. They said I had arthritis . . .
>
> (29-year-old male casual user)

Users were also quizzed as to whether cocaine had harmed or improved their work, relationships, and finances. Some 42 per cent claimed that cocaine had improved the quality of their work, and four chose to offer an explanation:

> It's, let me apply myself a wee bit more . . . no distractions: concentrate a wee bit better . . . you seem to home in on things better.'
>                          (29-year-old male casual user)

> I found it helpful in my public relations work, just as long as I didn't go over the score [overindulge] with it.
>                          (38-year-old male casual user)

> It enhances certain types of perception.
>                          (30-year-old female casual user)

> In our work [part of roadie team for travelling rock band] it's the people who don't use who are isolated and on the edge of things.
>                          (21-year-old female casual user)

A further 21 per cent claimed that their cocaine use had harmed the quality of their work, and this included 9 users who had previously indicated that cocaine had also improved the quality of their work. There are a number of published accounts of individuals using cocaine in their working lives, believing it initially to be a great assistance (particularly in creative activity) before later realising that the assistance rapidly becomes – if it was not always – an illusion if not an oppression, so this is not altogether surprising and should not be treated as contradictory.

Broadly similarly, 48 per cent claimed that their cocaine use had improved their relationship with their partner, and 23 per cent that it had harmed their relationship with their partner. Again, 11 respondents claimed that both were the case, and again, this isn't particularly surprising. One man chose to comment on cocaine's beneficial effect:

> In several ways problems are talked through, and we get on with each other's friends . . . [but for cocaine] we might not have this.
>                          (28-year-old male casual user)

Respondents were also asked if their cocaine use had harmed them financially, and over a third (34 per cent) agreed. Some seemed to feel they could control their expenditure on cocaine:

> Price isn't important, and has nothing to do with the amount taken.
>                          (26-year-old female casual user)

If I can't afford something, I do without it.
>                                 (28-year-old male casual user)

I've never really felt the need to spend money I don't have on coke.
>                                 (32-year-old male casual user)

As many claimed that the financial harm was very real:

Yes, I've blown £80 in one go . . . and regretted it afterwards.
>                                 (27-year-old male casual user)

I once had to get myself an overdraft.
>                                 (40-year-old male intensive user)

It harmed me in that my husband sold some, got into trouble and hence prison.
>                                 (24-year-old female ceased user)

Finally, respondents were asked what less-than-ideal activities they had ever indulged in to get cocaine. Here, 39 per cent said that they had spent time with people they didn't like to get cocaine, 34 per cent that they had borrowed money to get cocaine, 13 per cent that they had sold cocaine to get some for their own use, 5 per cent that they had sold possessions, 4 per cent that they had got an extra job, 3 per cent that they had taken things from family or friends, and 2 per cent that they had 'traded sex' for cocaine (one woman, and one man).

## PORTRAITS

As a way of sketching out 'typical' cocaine use in Scotland within this group of users (whose relationship to all those who use cocaine in Scotland is unknown) we have taken the modal values for all variables for both men and women in the group to suggest statistical norms for these mostly 'invisible' cocaine users.

Modal Scottish Cocaine Using Man is aged 27, and has lived with his partner for more than a year. He completed his education at university, where he obtained a degree. He is currently working as a sound and vision equipment operator, and earns between £10 001 and £15 000 a year. He's used many illegal drugs in his time – amphetamines, cannabis, opiates, hallucinogens, and tranquillisers – but he has never used crack. Apart from cocaine the only other drug he's used in the last three months is cannabis, but he would use amphetamines, cannabis and hallucinogens if offered them free.

He's never had a drug-related illness or been convicted of any offence related to his use of drugs. He knows five other people who use cocaine, three of whom are male. Actually, he hasn't used cocaine more than five times in the last three years, but would use some again if offered it free.

He likes cocaine because it makes him more energetic, and better at communicating. It increases his self-confidence, and makes him feel both relaxed and more creative. For him, it prolongs sex and makes it more pleasurable, and generally increases feelings of excitement. However, he thinks cocaine is too expensive, and leads to sleeplessness and insomnia. He doesn't agree that cocaine creates psychological dependence, or makes him irritated or depressed, nor does it have any unpleasant physical side effects.

He first snorted cocaine five years ago when he was 22 and visiting a friend in England, and was offered it free in the friend's house, although he hadn't asked for it. In the year that followed, he used cocaine less than once a month, always snorting, and usually only a couple of 'lines' when he did so.

However, when he was 23, he consumed rather more during what he now refers to as a four-month 'heavy' period, when he was snorting up to four lines not on a daily basis, but more often than once a week. He has most recently gone back to taking cocaine less than once a month, and only about two lines on each occasion. Looking back, he would say that his cocaine career was one where his use of cocaine increased gradually until it reached a peak, from whence it has since decreased.

Modal Scottish Cocaine Using Woman is currently a year younger at 26, but has also lived with her partner for more than a year. She completed her education at school, which she left after obtaining Highers (equivalent to English 'A' Levels). She is currently working as a dress designer, and also earns between £10 001 and £15 000 a year. She's used a fair number of illegal drugs in her time too – amphetamines, cannabis, opiates, hallucinogens, and tranquillisers – but she has also never used crack.

Apart from cocaine the other drugs she's used in the last three months are amphetamines and cannabis, and she would use amphetamines, cannabis and hallucinogens if offered them free.

She knows ten other people who use cocaine, more than he does, and seven of them are women. She's never had a drug-related illness or been convicted of any offence related to her use of drugs. Funnily enough, she's used cocaine far more times than him (11 to 30 times) in the last three years, and she too would use some again if offered some free. Like him, she likes cocaine because it makes her more energetic, and better at communicating. It increases her self-confidence, and makes her feel both relaxed and more creative.

For her, too, cocaine prolongs sex and makes it more pleasurable, and generally increases feelings of excitement. However, she thinks cocaine is too expensive, and leads to sleeplessness and insomnia. She doesn't agree that cocaine creates psychological dependence, or that it has any unpleasant physical side-effects. Unlike him, she does think cocaine makes her irritated and depressed.

She first snorted cocaine five years earlier when she was 21 and visiting a friend in Edinburgh. She, too, was offered it free in the friend's house, and she hadn't asked for it either. In the year that followed, she used cocaine less than once a month, always snorting, and usually only one 'line' when she did so. However, two years after she first used cocaine, when she was 23, she began a 4-month 'heavy' period, when she didn't snort any more than the one line she was accustomed to, but now began to do it every day.

She has now gone back to doing cocaine less than once a month, and still only about one line on each occasion. Looking back, she would say that her cocaine career was one of extremely varied use of cocaine over time.

These two people are statistical fictions. Here, finally, is a real user. A 32-year-old Scottish man, who has been a regular cocaine user for some years. He thinks he knows what he is talking about, and he has the grace not to be sure:

> Addictive? a bit of a silly question really, because it seems to put cocaine on the same par as heroin, and I've never found coke to be particularly addictive . . . certainly not addictive enough to bother me when I don't have it . . . anyone who says coke is addictive is talking bullshit. It's a very greedy sort of drug, that's all.

REFERENCES

Biernacki, P., and Waldorf, D. (1981) 'Snowball Sampling: Problems and Techniques of Chair Referral Sampling', *Sociological Methods and Research*, 10, pp. 141–63.
Chitwood, D. D. and Morningstar, P. C. (1985) 'Factors which differentiate

cocaine users in treatment from nontreatment users', *International Journal of the Addictions*, 20, pp. 449–59.

Cohen, P. (1989) *Cocaine Use in Amsterdam in Non-Deviant Subcultures*, Amsterdam: Instituut voor Sociale Geografie.

Ditton, J. *et al.* (1991) 'Scottish Cocaine Users: Wealthy Snorters or Delinquent Smokers' *Drug and Alcohol Dependence* 28 (December), pp. 269–76.

Ditton, Jason and Speirits, Kevin, (1981) 'The Rapid Increase of Heroin Addiction in Glasgow during 1981', *Background Paper*, Sociology Department, Glasgow University.

Erickson, P., Adalf, E., and Petrie, W (1987) *The Steel Drug: Cocaine in Perspective* (Toronto: Lexington).

Hammersley, R. H. (1990) 'The menace of the war on crack in Britain', *International Journal on Drug Policy*, 2, pp. 28–30.

Hammersley, R. H., Forsyth, A. J. M., Morrison, V. and Davies, J. B. (1989) 'The relationship between crime and opioid use', *British Journal of Addiction*, 84, pp. 1029–43.

Hammersley, R. H., Lavelle, T. L. and Forsyth, A. J. M. (1990) 'Buprenorphine and temazepam abuse', *British Journal of Addiction* 85, pp. 301–3.

Johnston, L. D., O'Malley, P. M. and Bachman, J. G. (1986) *Drug Use among American High School Students, College Students and Other Young Adults. National trends through 1985* (Rockville, MD:NIDA).

Kleber, H. D. (1988) 'Epidemic cocaine abuse: America's present, Britain's future?' *British Journal of Addiction*, 83, pp. 1359–71.

Morrison, V. and Plant, M. (1990) 'Drug problems and patterns of service use amongst illicit drug users in Edinburgh', *British Journal of Addiction*, 85, pp. 547–54.

Mugford, S. and Cohen, P. (1989) *Drug Use, Social Relations and Commodity Consumption: A Study of Recreational Cocaine Users in Sydney, Canberra and Melbourne*, Report to Research into Drug Abuse Advisory Committee, National Campaign Against Drug Abuse.

Pearson, Geoffrey (1987) *The New Heroin Users* (London: Blackwell).

Plant, M. A., Peck, D. F., and Samuel, E. (1985) *Alcohol, Drugs and School-leavers* (London: Tavistock).

US Department of State (1984) 'Trafficking and Misuse of Cocaine', Working Paper prepared for the Council of Europe Meeting by the Bureau of International Narcotics Matters, Washington.

# 5 Cocaine in Context: Findings from a South London Inner-City Drug Survey

Geoffrey Pearson, Heidi Safia Mirza and Stewart Phillips

This chapter is based on a survey of drug users known to a variety of different agencies in the south London borough of Lewisham. This is an area of London which has gained much notoriety through reports in the local and national press about certain housing estates said to be dealing centres for the crack–cocaine trade. Indeed, as a result of a sensational feature article in *The Sunday Times* (15 January 1989) entitled 'Hooked on Crack', the Milton Court estate in the Deptford area of north Lewisham was dubbed 'Crack City'. It had been further implied – not only by media coverage, but also by a certain amount of local rumour and gossip – that the drug problem in Lewisham was a black problem

The Drug Information Project had been set in motion in 1990 with Home Office funding through the Lewisham Safer Cities Project, in order to conduct a six-month survey of drug misuse in the borough which might clarify the nature and scale of the local drug problem. Given the encircling climate of debate, the local Safer Cities steering group requested that the survey should give specific attention to issues of race and gender.

The general outcomes of the survey are already available (Mirza, Pearson and Phillips, 1991). In a nutshell, we found that there is an extensive pattern of drug misuse in Lewisham. However, it is not primarily a cocaine or crack problem, and it does not predominantly involve black people. Rather, the most serious evidence of drug misuse is a result of the legacy of Britain's heroin epidemic of the 1980s.

This is hardly surprising. Earlier in the 1980s, the neighbouring borough of Southwark had attracted considerable notoriety as a centre of the heroin epidemic associated with the novel practice of 'chasing the dragon'. As Angela Burr's (1987 and 1989) research has shown, heroin misuse in this part of south London was part of a familiar pattern of urban poverty and delinquent lifestyles. Moreover, on all the available evidence the heroine epidemic of the 1980s had largely involved white people – whether in London or other parts of the country such as the North of England and Scotland where heroin misuse had become a major social difficulty (Pearson, Gilman and McIver, 1985 and 1986; Pearson, 1987a: Dorn and South, 1987; Parker, Bakx and Newcombe, 1988).

Nevertheless, cocaine and crack are certainly not unknown in south London. Local drug agency workers had been anxiously monitoring the situation for some time, and had formed the clear impression that although cocaine and crack had not assumed the form of a major local difficulty they were seeing increasing numbers of clients with problems related to cocaine, including its smokeable freebase form (Tippell and Aston, 1990; Southwark Drug Misuse Consultative Group, 1989). There is also evidence of increasing numbers of drug users known to the Community Drug Team at the Maudsley Hospital in Southwark who had used cocaine in its smokeable form (Strang, Griffiths and Gossop, 1990). Although the Drug Information Project cannot provide evidence on trends of drug misuse in Lewisham – in that it was essentially a 'snap-shot' survey – it does confirm that substantial numbers of heroin users are also known to smoke, inhale or inject cocaine as part of their repertoire of poly-drug use. Even so, the large majority of cocaine and crack users known to agencies are white drug users, reflecting the more general tendency for black people to be under-represented among drug users who seek help from drug services (Awiah, Butt and Dorn, 1990 and 1992).

The plan of this chapter is first to describe the background to the Drug Information Project. Then, there will be a brief discussion of the research strategy adopted and the broad outlines of the survey findings. In subsequent sections, the specific character of cocaine and crack use revealed by the survey will be addressed, with particular attention to the question of 'race' and the major differences which appeared in the survey outcomes between the kinds of cocaine and crack users known to the police and helping agencies.

## LEWISHAM: AN INNER-CITY MOSAIC

Lewisham is an inner London borough with a population of almost one-quarter of a million people, situated in the south-east of the metropolis. It is a multi-racial borough where 13 per cent of households were identified in the 1981 census as black, consisting predominantly of people of Afro-Caribbean descent. More recent estimates of population trends suggest that as many as 20 per cent of Lewisham's population in the 20–30 years age group might be black. There is also a sizeable Turkish community in Lewisham, although statistically this appears to be almost 'invisible'.

Lewisham is in many respects a divided borough. Bordered to the north by the River Thames, its northernmost areas of Deptford and New Cross are characterised by urban deprivation and decay, while to the south Lewisham stretches towards a more leafy and affluent suburban landscape. There are, however, many subtle variations which confound this broad characterisation of a north–south divide within the borough. For example, the south of the borough includes some extensive postwar municipal housing estates where there are significant pockets of social deprivation. Nevertheless, the north–south divide remain an accessible way of thinking about the borough, and its five most socially deprived electoral wards are tightly grouped together in the north of Lewisham (Hyde, Balloch and Ainley, 1990). Three of these count among the most deprived localities in the entire London area (Townsend, 1987).

Deptford itself has a rich cultural and commercial history, as the centre of Europe's major naval dockyard, established at the time of Henry VIII, although it is now no more than a picturesque detail of historical interest that Queen Elizabeth I came to Deptford Creek in order to confer a knighthood on Sir Francis Drake. Perhaps more to the point is that nearby is 'The Den', home of Millwall Football Club, whose supporters had adopted as their mournful chant, 'We Are Millwall. No one Likes Us, We Don't Care'. In fact, Millwall FC did care, and now counts among the leaders of community-based football initiatives in an inner-city context – including a successful women's team (Lightbown, 1990).

The naval dockyards had closed in the nineteenth century and, although the docks continued for many years as a centre for the foreign cattle market, the area's links with its dockland past are now completely severed. Deptford suffered major bomb damage during the Second World War, and the area was extensively redeveloped from the 1960s onwards, resulting in a typical inner-city panorama of high-rise housing estates, interspersed with tracts of derelict wasteland. It is in this northern area of Deptford and New Cross that Lewisham's black population is most densely concentrated. This is also a part of south London which for many years has attracted the sporadic attention of the National Front. Indeed, it was here in January 1981 that a fire which broke out at a household party caused the tragic deaths of thirteen young black people, injuring many more, resulting in a bitter controversy as to whether the fire had been an accident or had been the result of an attack by white racialists. In an account of the Deptford fire, Smith and Gray (1985, p. 429) take the view that the repercussions of the tragedy caused 'widespread damage to relations between the police and black people in London' and that 'it seems reasonable to assume that this added substantially to the tensions underlying the riots of April in the same year'.

As if Deptford did not already have enough problems, in the past few years it has attracted a large amount of media attention and police activity with a focus on drug-dealing. As already indicated, in January 1989 *The Sunday Times* had described the Milton Court housing estate as 'Crack City', allegedly a centre for crack–cocaine manufacture and distribution. The association was also made, both in the tabloid and 'quality' press that the 'crack' problem was a black problem. *The New Statesman* (3 February 1989) had followed this lead, carrying 'Crack City' as its front-page feature article, although there was some attempt to offset the problem of drug-dealing against a more general picture of urban deprivation: 'The Milton Court Estate is, for the media, the centre of the British crack industry. Drugs there are. But the residents worry more about leaking roofs, piss in the lifts and the public squalor of the 1980s.'

Attention had first been drawn to 'Crack City' by a widely-publicised police raid in November 1988 when oxyacetylene torches and a hydraulic device had been used to break into a flat which had been fortified by a steel door, and where baking powder and other paraphernalia had provided evidence that a 'crack factory' had been located in the kitchen. What had been more immediately observable on the estate, however, was that an open space nearby the Spanish Steps pub was a hang-out for minor drug-dealing – in all probability mainly cannabis. Following the police raid in November 1988, media attention had focused on the 'crack factory' slant of the news story and Milton Court had begun to gather to itself a novel kind of notoriety.

According to *The Sunday Times* report, the estate had become a national centre for drug-dealing and, employing a well-tested vox-pop technique, it was alleged that it 'is known as "Crack City" by locals'. According to the social services team leader interviewed by the *The New Statesman*, however, this allegation was rejected as 'nonsense': 'The first time I ever came across the phrase "Crack City" was in the *Sunday Times*'.

A subsequent survey of crime and housing conditions on the Milton Court estate, carried out by the Safe Neighbourhoods Unit and commissioned by the Lewisham Safer Cities Project, offered a broader context in which to situate this catalogue of controversy and complaint. It was felt that *The Sunday Times* had painted 'a lurid picture . . . of a crime-ridden inner city ghetto with widespread drug dealing, gratuitous violence and racial tension'; and that where the *New Stateman* was concerned, 'although critical of *The Sunday Times* hyperbole', it 'sustained the image of a fearful and demoralised population of a poorly managed and under-resourced estate' (Safe Neighbourhoods Unit, 1990, p. 10).

For its part, the Safe Neighbourhoods Unit confirmed that there were 'serious levels of poverty' on Milton Court, and that residents did experience 'problems in respect of personal safety and the security of their homes'. Even so, it was found that confidence in the police was 'comparatively high', with most discontent with police performance found among those aged 16–30 years, the age group which was also most worried about the risk of burglary (Safe Neighbourhood Unit, pp. 50, 58).

Where drug-dealing was concerned, the Safe Neighbourhoods Unit reported that it had assumed the proportions of a major problem during the summer of 1989. Gatherings of dealers and buyers near the local pub and outside the entrance lobbies to tower-blocks had become a considerable nuisance and source of anxiety to local residents, whereupon the police had initiated a low-profile enforcement operation. Fearful that 'a heavy-handed clean-up operation might provoke public disorder', the police had adopted a strategy of deterring buyers in the locality by making arrests away from the estate: a strategy of deterrence aimed at reducing demand which has been tried elsewhere by the Metropolitan Police, including the All Saints Road in Notting Hill. As a consequence, it was said that the drug problem on Milton Court had been much reduced in scale.

Even so, worries about drugs still loomed large among residents' concerns when asked by the Safe Neighbourhoods Unit to identify 'big' problems on the estate. Judged by these responses Milton Court appeared as a sadly typical inner-city estate where residents – and particularly those living in high-rise tower blocks – identified as the major problems in their lives questions of unemployment, vandalism, graffiti, crime, drugs and the estate's reputation. It goes without saying that the estate's reputation had hardly been improved by the loving attentions of journalists on the staff of *The Sunday Times*.

The Drug Information Project was scheduled to start in April 1990, and only a few weeks before this there was another widely-publicised police operation on a Deptford housing estate involving 130 officers when crack was seized, together with other drugs. The British press was also gearing itself up for the World Ministerial Drug Summit, to be hosted by Mrs Thatcher in London. Among other news coverage, Britain's major black newspaper *The Voice* (3 April 1990) carried a front-page headline. 'COCAINE: Britain's Inner-City Crisis. We Must Act Now to Halt the Misery'. Announcing that it was 'declaring war on the pushers', in its editorial comment *The Voice* declared that 'there is no escaping the simple fact that we have become too complacent and accepting of drug use amongst us. For many marijuana has for a long time been accepted as an everyday social drug like alcohol. Now it seems cocaine is going the same way.' Turning its attention once again to a Deptford housing estate, the magazine section of *The Sunday Times* (1 April 1990) carried a front-page feature article: 'On the Streets of Britain Today: Crack for Sale'. In addition to stark photographic evidence of black suspects being searched and handcuffed during the Deptford police raid, *The Sunday Times* carried the 'personal guarantee' by Mr Bob Stutman of the US Drug Enforcement Agency that 'the UK would be swamped by crack'. It was therefore against a somewhat agitated background of controversy that our research was set in motion.


## THE MAIN SURVEY FINDINGS: REVEALING CRACKS IN THE 'CRACK CITY' MYTH

The central aim of our research was to collate information from a variety of agencies – including specialist drug agencies, the probation service, the social services department, and the police – about those people known to them who were illicit drug users. The method was an adaptation of the 'multi-agency enumeration' strategy developed by the Drug Indicators Project at Birkbeck College in the University of London (Hartnoll *et al.*, 1985a and 1985b). Variations of this survey method have also been used by researchers in other parts of the British Isles, such as Glasgow, the Wirral peninsula in Merseyside, Tyneside, and Nottingham (Haw, 1985; Parker, Bakx and Newcombe, 1988; Pattison, Barnes and Thorley, 1982; Giggs *et al.*, 1989).

One difference in our approach was that, although this was certainly not the first time that a survey method of this kind had been employed in a multi-racial inner-city area, reflecting a tradition of 'race-shy' research, there has been a surprising neglect of issues of race and ethnicity in previous drugs research in Britain. Indeed, race has not been addressed at all in the published findings of other major survey ventures such as those in Wirral, Glasgow and Nottingham. In our case, as will already be clear, the question of race was both central and unavoidable.

In view of the short timescale of the Drug Information Project which aimed to provide a quick feedback to the Lewisham Safer Cities Project, it was also necessary to make some adaptations and abbreviations to the methodology. It was unrealistic, for example, to aim for a sound prevalence estimate of drug misuse in the borough. Our objective was more modest: to indicate the pattern of drug misuse known to a number of selected agencies, especially those working at the interface of health and social service delivery and the criminal justice system, so that, although extensive contacts were made with a wide variety of agencies which serve the borough of Lewisham, the range of agencies covered by the survey was not exhaustive. Where medical services were concerned, for example, only specialist drug services were involved in the survey, although consultation took place on a wider basis. Problem drug users who came to be known only through contact with generic medical service and primary health care systems, such as those provided by general practitioners and health visitors, were therefore not included in our survey data. Where specialist drug services were concerned, however, contacts were also made with agencies located outside the borough boundaries, revealing a substantial number of drug users resident in Lewisham who were known to these agencies.

One final consideration is that ideally, in a survey such as this, a uniform case-identification and counting procedure should be adopted. For example, it is customary to ask agencies to identify all problem drug users with whom they have had contact in the preceding twelve months. Although this condition was met in the majority of cases, it proved to be not always possible because of constraints on

agency resources, staff-turnover, different systems of protecting confidentiality, and variations in agency recording practices. Accordingly, it was necessary to relax our requirement of a uniform information
retrieval system in some instances.

In the case of the Inner London Probation Service, for example,
the ILPS Demonstration Unit had only recently completed a snap-
shot survey of drug users known to probation officers in the whole of
inner London (ILPS, 1990). It was clearly unrealistic under these
circumstances, and in view of the pressure on staff resources, to
request probation officers to complete yet another questionnaire. In
this instance, we were provided with the ILPS Demonstration Unit's
data base for the Lewisham area which proved to be largely compatible with our requirements. We also negotiated a three-month
through-put study of all new cases involving drug misuse coming to
the notice of the probation service in the Lewisham area.

Where the social services department was concerned, problems
with the recruitment and retention of social work staff – a general
difficulty in the London area – meant that owing to high rates of
staff-turnover it would not always be possible for area terms to
provide a twelve-month review of cases without an exceptionally
heavy investment of time and effort. In these cases a snap-shot survey
was requested. The routine workloads of social workers are such that
a snap-shot was in all likelihood an adequate measure of the agency's
workload, since most social work staff time is directed towards long-
term work in the areas of childcare and child protection. A through-
put study of social work duty teams would, however, have been
unrealistic given both resource pressures and the unlikelihood that
social workers on intake teams would be aware of a person's drug
habits. Such a procedure might even deter people from referring
themselves to social services duty teams, if they were quizzed about
their drug use in a routine way.

Our response to these difficulties was therefore one of pragmatism.
It seemed both more realistic, and potentially more helpful, to adjust
our approach in such a way that it reflected the routine working
practices, resource difficulties and recording systems of different
agencies – rather than to attempt to impose a uniform monitoring
system on all agencies.

The questionnaire employed for data collection was designed in a
user-friendly manner, occupying one side of A4 paper, together with
a further page of instructions and guidance. Its format had been fully
negotiated with all participating agencies. It asked first for the in-

itials, sex, month and date of birth, and residential postcode for each client known to the agency. This information provided a confidential personal identification for each drug user which allowed us to avoid double-counting where a person was known to more than one agency. Additional information was requested on the person's occupational status, housing tenure, household composition, whether there were dependent children in the household, and race/ethnic background. The ethnic coding employed was: White; Afro-Caribbean; Asian; Other Ethnic Group. The vast majority of Lewisham's black population are of Afro-Caribbean descent and, reflecting this, only a tiny number of people were identified as Asian or Other Ethnic Group. Accordingly, for the purposes of the survey analysis we adopted a simple black/white distinction.

Finally, agencies were asked to provide information on the individual's known pattern of drug use and whether or not drugs were injected. Tick-off boxes were provided for the following categories of drug: heroin; methadone; cocaine; amphetamines; tranquillisers; cannabis; with a space to specify other substances used. Agencies were also asked to identify the main drug used, together with the length of time of main drug use. In this way, we were able to identify both patterns of Main Drug Use and All Drugs Used, thus offering information on styles of poly-drug use. This proved to be particularly important where cocaine and crack use was concerned. Very little cocaine or crack use was identified as the main drug used, although there was a substantial amount of cocaine and crack use by poly-drug users for whom the primary drug of use was heroin.

In total, returns were received from agencies identifying 1115 individual drug users known to them. Of these, 65 cases were eliminated either on the grounds that the drug user lived outside Lewisham, or because the questionnaire had not been completed in a useable form. A small number of cases were also eliminated in order to avoid double-counting, either because the individual was known to more than one agency, or had been arrested more than once by the police in the same time period. However, a surprisingly small number of problem drug users were known to more than one agency.

Our survey data therefore covered 1050 cases of whom 580 were known to be using 'notifiable' drugs. This figure contrasts with 179 drug users identified in the most recent statistics available from the Home Office/Department of Health notification index for the Lewisham and North Southwark District Health Authority in the period January to December 1989 (Department of Health, 1990). Given that the District Health Authority covers a wider geographical area than the Borough of Lewisham, strict comparisons are not possible. Nevertheless, it is reasonable to estimate that the Drug Information Project identified at least four times as many drug users in the Lewisham area than are recorded in the official notification index.

Of these 1050 cases, 45 per cent were known to specialist drug agencies. Voluntary sector drug agencies accounted for the lion's share of these, amounting to 39 per cent of the total sample. A further 39 per cent of cases were the result of arrests by different branches of the Metropolitan Police, 10 per cent were known to the probation service, and 6 per cent were identified by the social services department.

In terms of the social characteristics of the overall sample, two-thirds of known drug users were unemployed: and of those in employment, two-thirds were involved in either manual occupations or the service sector. A further 9 per cent were self-employed in a wide variety of occupations (ranging from businessman to busker and prostitute) and 7 per cent were of professional status. Slightly more than one-half of the sample were living in local authority housing, with one-fifth in private rented accommodation and one-tenth living in owner-occupied housing. A further one-fifth of the sample were either homeless, in care, in custody or squatting.

In terms of household composition, one-fifth were living alone, one-quarter were living with parents, 16 per cent were sharing accommodation with others, and 40 per cent were living with a partner. One-third of known drug users were estimated to have dependent children, although not all agencies provided answers to this question. Those which did included most of the specialist drug services, probation and the social services department. Among those drug users identified as having responsibility for children by these agencies, 70 per cent were heroin or opiate users.

Finally, we turn to questions of age, race and gender. Not surprisingly, slightly more than one-half of all identified drug users were aged between 20 and 29 years. One-tenth were aged 15–19 years, and a further 27 per cent were aged 30–39 years. Not much more than 5 per cent were forty years or older. In terms of the length of time of main drug use, one-half of identified drug users were known to have been using drugs for five years or less, and one-third had been using for three years or less. By comparison, one-third had been using for 10 years or more and one-tenth had been using for 15 years or more.

The racial coding employed by the research identified 79 per cent of the sample as white, and 19 per cent of Afro-Caribbean descent. Small numbers, each less than 1 per cent, were identified as Asian or of mixed parentage. Among the total sample, three-quarters of known drug users were men, which tends to reflect known national trends.

Before proceeding any further in this brief summary of the survey findings, however, it is as well to say that the kinds of drug users known to different agencies (and the kinds of drug that they were using) differed appreciably from one type of agency to another. Any attempt to interpret the overall survey findings without attention to these multi-agency variations therefore risks being deeply misleading. For example, whereas 90 per cent of police arrests involved men, one-half of drug users known to the social services department were women. Where specialist drug agencies are concerned, one-third of their clients were women. Equally, although 85–90 per cent of the clients of drug agencies were heroin users, less than 5 per cent of police arrests involved heroin. By comparison, although it was only rarely that people referred themselves to drug agencies with problems related to cannabis use, 80 per cent of police arrests involved cannabis – which follows a national trend whereby the vast bulk of arrests, cautions and convictions for drug offences in Britain are concerned with the unlawful possession of cannabis (Pearson, 1991a). Finally, where the question of 'race' is concerned, we are confronted by an irreconcilable difference between agency perceptions of the nature of the 'drug problem' in Lewisham. Whereas only 6 per cent of drug users known to specialist drug agencies were black, the Metropolitan Police appeared to be operating an exquisite equal opportunities policy whereby almost one-half of all arrests for drug offences involved black people.

It is therefore necessary to turn a blind eye to all manner of difficulties as one approaches the survey findings in their overall form. Taking a deep statistical breath, the most commonly-encountered form of drug misuse involved heroin or other opiates, which accounted for almost one-half of all main drug use. Cannabis (largely in the form of police arrests) accounted for a further one-third of the total sample of returns for main drug use. On this reckoning, cocaine and crack were almost out of sight: cocaine was identified as the main drug used in merely 4 per cent of cases, and crack in less than 3 per cent. Amphetamines and tranquillisers also amounted to less than 3 per cent and 4 per cent respectively. For the rest – in spite of the known increases in the recent popularity of LSD,

*Table* 5.1   main drug use and all drugs used: selected categories
(N = 1050)

|  | Main drug use Number | % | All drugs used Number | % | Injecting (%) |
|---|---|---|---|---|---|
| Heroin | 448 | 44 | 477 | 46 | 66 |
| Methadone | 50 | 5 | 248 | 24 | 13 |
| Cocaine | 43 | 4 | 165 | 16 | 30 |
| Crack | 29 | 3 | 85 | 8 | – |
| Amphetamine | 26 | 3 | 148 | 14 | 40 |
| Tranquilliser | 40 | 4 | 163 | 16 | 20 |
| LSD | 6 | 1 | 42 | 4 | – |
| Ecstasy | 4 | – | 11 | 1 | – |
| Cannabis | 351 | 34 | 671 | 64 | – |

Ecstasy and other 'recreational' drugs – these went almost unmentioned in terms of main drug use.

The analysis of all drugs used presents a somewhat different picture, reflecting the fact that most forms of illicit drug use involve patterns of poly-drug use (see Table 5.1). Here, cannabis is the most commonly-used drug – known to be used by 64 per cent of the total sample, a reflection of the widespread use of cannabis in contemporary Britain. Among class A drugs, heroin (46 per cent) remains the 'market leader', although methadone (24 per cent) also enters the picture more emphatically. Amphetamines (14 per cent of all drugs used) and tranquillisers (16 per cent) also assert their presence. Moreover, it is when we turn to all drugs used that we begin to glimpse the potential significance of cocaine and crack, which account for 16 per cent and 8 per cent of all drugs used.

Adding this admittedly fragmented evidence together, it is a reasonable conclusion that journalistic fables concerning 'Crack City' are not particularly helpful in attempting to understand the nature and scale of drug misuse in an inner-city community such as Lewisham. The most obvious evidence of a serious drug problem remains that of heroin misuse, where two-thirds of heroin users are known to be drug injectors.

Cocaine and crack, a point to be established in later sections of this chapter, mainly find their niche within patterns of poly-drug use where heroin is the main drug of use. Moreover, the vast majority of cocaine and crack users are white people who supplement their ration of opiates with a stimulant cocaine high: perhaps most often as a periodic recreational 'kick' or 'treat'. Opiate addiction becomes a dull routine after a period of time, and people who use heroin and other opiates will often attempt to bring some life into this daily treadmill by employing a variety of occasional stimulants or hallucinogenics – including not only amphetamines and cocaine, but also other more exotic substances such as travel-sickness preparations which contain the psycho-active ingredient cyclizine (Gilman and Pearson, 1991; Gilman, Traynor and Pearson, 1990).

The idea that the major drug problem facing an inner-city community such as Lewisham is a ghetto-dwelling black dope-fiend would appear to stand revealed as a myth. Even so, the association between drug misuse and social deprivation is not at all dispelled by the findings of the Drug Information Project. Research in both North America and Britain has repeatedly revealed those 'urban clustering' effects whereby heroin misuse comes to be most densely concentrated in areas of high unemployment and housing decay (Pearson, 1987b; Pearson and Gilman, 1992; Pearson, Gilman and McIver, 1986; Haw, 1985; Parker, Bakx and Newcombe, 1988; Giggs et al., 1989; Fazey, Brown and Batey, 1990). The pattern has been repeated within the USA crack epidemic of the 1980s, which has taken its most serious toll among black and Hispanic communities in the ghettoes of New York and elsewhere (Bourgois, 1989; Williams, 1989).

One highly significant finding of the Lewisham survey was that drug misuse is most densely concentrated in the northern parts of the borough which are characterised by the highest levels of social deprivation (Mirza, Pearson and Phillips, 1991, Table 8). On the basis of our survey data, the estimated rate of Class A drug use per 1000 population varies between 0.4 per thousand in one of the more affluent parts of Lewisham, to 5.2 per thousand in the northern part of the borough which includes Deptford. The estimated prevalence of Class A drug use therefore follows the steep gradients of social deprivation within Lewisham (Hyde, Balloch and Ainley, 1989). This northern area, it will be remembered, is also where a significantly higher proportion of black people live. Is this, then, final confirmation of the 'black' drug problem in Lewisham?

The simple answer is 'No'. Those readers accustomed to social research methodology will be familiar with the 'ecological fallacy', whereby it is invalid to infer from the findings of area surveys about the behaviour of individuals living within those areas (Robinson, 1950). For example, it cannot be assumed from an area survey which finds that drug use is concentrated in areas of high unemployment that drug users are invariably unemployed people. In the case of the Lewisham survey, we have a splendid example of the ecological fallacy. Although Class A drug misuse is more densely concentrated in the northern parts of Lewisham, where black people are more likely to live, the drug users who predominantly account for this area effect are white heroin users.


BLACK AND WHITE: COCAINE AND CRACK USERS KNOWN TO HELPING AGENCIES

Having set cocaine in its wider context, we can examine the specific findings of the nature of cocaine and crack use revealed by the Drug Information Project. It will be useful to do this step-by-step, first examining white cocaine users and then black cocaine users. This is not done for any reasons of methodological 'apartheid'. Rather, it is both because the issue of cocaine–crack use within the black community had assumed such prominence in local discussions on the supposed nature of the cocaine problem, and also by virtue of a number of significant differences which emerged between black and white cocaine users. The discussion is also initially restricted to cocaine and crack users known to helping agencies – that is, drug services, the probation service, and the social services department. A consideration of police statistics, and a comparison between police arrests and drug users known to helping agencies, is to be found in the following section. The reasons for this approach will become clear. But first some words of introduction.

Cocaine use is not new in Britain. Quite apart from its earlier history in the late nineteenth and early twentieth centuries, in the 1960s London's drug users commonly injected cocaine in combination with heroin in a so-called 'speedball' (Stimson and Oppenheimer, 1982). Cocaine has never quite lost its image as a 'champagne' drug, however, and its street price has tended to remain high. Correspondingly, in the 1970s and 1980s amphetamines (known as 'speed' or 'whizz', and which were much cheaper) were also more popular as a recreational stimulant drug.

Where 'crack' is concerned, although the word itself is new, there is also a substantial amount of anecdotal evidence among drug users and drug professionals in south London (and elsewhere) that techniques of smoking freebase cocaine have been known and practised for many years by some drug users. Indeed, we found that the use of the word 'crack' to describe the practice of smoking cocaine could cause some confusion in London. It is not only that people who use cocaine in this way are more likely to refer to 'freebase', 'wash' or 'rock'. The term 'crack', which follows one specific form of usage from the USA cocaine epidemic of the 1980s, has also come to be associated with dramatic portrayals from the USA of street-warfare. To employ the word 'crack' in London in 1990, therefore, sometimes led to disbelief or denial. It could either be taken to be associated with press sensationalism, where south London had been a major focus, or to be describing something entirely new and unprecedented. To offer one example of such a response, a black youth worker dismissed talk about 'crack' (understood as a novel threat) by saying that, 'Cocaine's been around for ages, mainly in cigarettes.'

As already indicated, on the basis of the DIP survey the use of smokeable freebase cocaine (that is, 'crack') would appear to remain a minority pursuit among known drug users. Even so, it is possible that the survey evidence fails to reveal the true amount of crack use (even among known drug-users) by virtue of the linguistic confusions already mentioned. Although the DIP questionnaire distinguished between 'crack' and 'cocaine' use, it is possible that some people identified as 'cocaine' users were smoking the drug. Approximately one-third of cocaine users were known to be injecting cocaine, but it cannot be readily assumed that the remaining two-thirds were all inhaling ('snorting') cocaine powder.

Having set out these qualifications to our findings, we will now describe them in more detail. It has already been indicated that the vast bulk of cocaine and crack use was found within a context of poly-drug use where the main drug used was heroin or another opiate. In overall terms, approximately one-fifth of drug users identified by agencies other than the police, were known to use cocaine while slightly less than one-tenth had used crack, some of whom were reported to be using both crack and cocaine. This overall finding would appear to be entirely consistent with the monitoring of cocaine use in south London by the Community Drug Team at the Maudsley Hospital between 1987 and 1989. Whereas 92 per cent of the patients seen identified opiates as their main problem drug and only 1 per cent were primarily cocaine users, 18 per cent had used cocaine in the month prior to their assessment (Strang, Griffiths and Gossop, 1990). It is also noticeable that while the proportion of cocaine users in the Maudsley sample who smoked the drug, rather than injecting or inhaling it, was found to be increasing over this three-year period, it

*Table* 5.2   White cocaine/heroin poly-drug users known to drug agencies
(N = 93)

|  | Cocaine | Crack | Cocaine and crack |
|---|---|---|---|
| Male IVDUs | 41 (78%) | 8 (38%) | 16 (69%) |
| Female IVDUs | 21 (71%) | 3 (100%) | 4 (100%) |
| Total IVDUs | 62 (76%) | 11 (55%) | 20 (75%) |

remained true that 75 per cent of these cocaine users were white. In our own sample, a total of 161 people were identified as cocaine or crack users by helping agencies of whom the majority (n = 111) were known to drug agencies. Among all cocaine and crack users known to helping agencies, 80 per cent were white.

A total of 130 white cocaine and crack users were known to helping agencies, of whom the large majority were again known to specialist drug agencies. Indeed, one local 'street agency' accounted for 42 of these: one-third of all white cocaine and crack users, and slightly more than 40 per cent of those known to drug agencies.

Where drug agencies were concerned, 101 white clients were known to be using either cocaine and/or crack. Of these, only eight people (four men and four women) were primarily cocaine or crack users. The remaining 93 cases were all using cocaine or its crack derivative in combination with heroin which was usually their main drug of use. A handful of people were specifically identified as equally devoted to cocaine and heroin, and in two cases their heroin use was believed to have been subsequent to their cocaine or crack use. In summary, approximately 30 per cent of white heroin users known to drug agencies were either using cocaine or crack.

The drug use profiles of these 93 poly-drug users known to be using cocaine can be broken down into more detail (see Table 5.2). More than two-thirds (70 per cent) were men, which is not too different from the overall gender profile of the white clientele of these agencies, of whom 65 per cent were men. Two-thirds (n = 62) were using cocaine only in combination with heroin, of whom 76 per cent were intravenous drug users. A further one-fifth (n = 20) were using both cocaine and crack in combination with heroin, of whom 75 per cent were IVDUs. Finally, slightly more than one-tenth (n = 11) were smoking crack in combination with heroin, of whom 55 per cent were IVDUs. Overall, 73 per cent of these white cocaine–crack-using poly-drug users were IVDUs, and one-third of them were definitely known to be injecting cocaine as well as heroin.

A smaller number (n = 29) of white cocaine users were also known to the probation service and the local social services department. Once again, a pattern of poly-drug use was predominant and in only seven cases did cocaine or crack appear to be the sole drug used. This small sub-sample must be treated with some care, in that it might be subject to different degrees of unreliability. Evidence on patterns of drug misuse supplied by probation and social services is invariably and understandably less reliable than that provided by drug services. This is because, even if the social and personal difficulties experienced by the clients of these services are drug-related, the reasons for self-referral or intervention in their lives are much less likely to have a direct drug focus. Indeed, a client might sometimes attempt to conceal their drug misuse from probation officers and social workers. It seems generally true, moreover, that although substantial proportions of the clients of the probation service are known to have drug or alcohol related problems, drug problems appear to make much less of an impact on the routine workloads of social workers in social service departments (ILPS, 1990; Laister & Pearson, 1988). It is not clear whether this is because social workers actually have less routine contact with problem drug users, or if social workers fail to recognise these problems. In view of the considerable emphasis given to child protection in the workloads of social workers, for example, it is widely acknowledged that clients will attempt to conceal patterns of illicit drug use for fear that their children might be taken into public care (Pearson, 1991b). A further complication in the Drug Information Project sample is that where the probation service is concerned, our data collection relied upon a survey recently conducted by the Inner London Probation Service which was not strictly compatible with our questionnaire format, in that the ILPS data did not distinguish between cocaine use and crack use (ILPS, 1990).

In spite of these qualifications, the white cocaine users identified by probation and social services did not appear to be substantially different from those known to drug agencies. Of the 29 cases notified, 17 came from the probation service and 12 from social services. Among cocaine-using probation clients, reflecting the general characteristics of probation caseloads, all but two were men; where social services were concerned, five out of twelve were women. The large majority of the probation/social services sample (80 per cent) were poly-drug users for whom the main drug used was heroin. Of these, 85 per cent were IVDUs. Where social services were concerned, crack use was identified in the majority of cases (9 out of 12) which is perhaps the only way in which this sub-sample differed from the cocaine users known to drug services. As already indicated, data supplied by the probation service did not always distinguish between cocaine use and crack use, although the vast majority (13 out of 17 cases) were known to be injecting cocaine, all of whom were poly-drug injectors.

We can compare this profile of the white cocaine or crack user with those black people known to agencies who were using cocaine or crack (see Table 5.3). Overall, 70 per cent of all black people known to helping agencies who were using Class A drugs (n = 45) were using heroin, which is not too dissimilar to the pattern of drug misuse among white users. However, a larger proportion of black drug users (70 per cent as against 30 per cent for whites) were known to be using either crack or cocaine. Moreover, although the majority of black cocaine and crack users (55 per cent) were poly-drug users who used cocaine or crack in combination with heroin, this poly-drug use trend was less pronounced than where white cocaine users were concerned. Indeed, almost one-third of black drug users known to agencies were primarily cocaine or crack users whereas only one-tenth of white drug users were primarily cocaine or crack users.

Equally marked was the decreased likelihood that black drug users were IVDUs. Whereas almost 70 per cent of white drug users known to be using cocaine were IVDUs (the figure rises to 75 per cent for those people employing patterns of poly-drug use) for black drug users the figure was little more than 15 per cent. Moreover, no black women who used cocaine were drug injectors, although a small number of black women were known to inject heroin who did not use either cocaine or crack. This contrasts with approximately 80 per cent of white women with a pattern of heroin/cocaine poly-drug use who were injectors. These marked differences between the proportions of drug injectors among white and black people known to agencies were also reflected in the fact that among all Class A drug use by black people only 30 per cent injected drugs, as opposed to approximately 70 per cent of the much larger group of white Class A drug users who were IVDUs.

What reliable conclusions can be drawn from this comparison of white and black cocaine users known to helping agencies? Agency

*Table* 5.3(i)  Cocaine and crack users known to helping agencies by race

|  | Black | % IVDU | White | % IVDU |
|---|---|---|---|---|
| All cocaine/crack use | 31 | 16% | 130 | 69% |
| Heroin and cocaine/crack | 17 | 24% | 115 | 75% |
| Cocaine/crack alone | 14 | 7% | 15 | 20% |

*Table* 5.3(ii)  White cocaine and crack users known to helping agencies by sex

|  | Male | % IVDU | Female | % IVDU |
|---|---|---|---|---|
| All cocaine/crack use | 91 | 69% | 39 | 67% |
| Heroin and cocaine/crack | 82 | 73% | 33 | 79% |
| Cocaine/crack alone | 9 | 33% | 6 | 0% |

*Table* 5.3(iii)  Black cocaine and crack users known to helping agencies by sex

|  | Male | % IVDU | Female | % IVDU |
|---|---|---|---|---|
| All cocaine/crack use | 25 | 20% | 6 | 0% |
| Heroin and cocaine/crack | 14 | 29% | 3 | 0% |
| Cocaine/crack alone | 11 | 9% | 3 | 0% |

records themselves cannot provide a basis on which to infer the overall character of cocaine and crack use in the Lewisham area. They can only describe the pattern of drug misuse among people who refer themselves, or are referred, for help. The fact that fewer black clients are known to agencies, for example, does not mean that drug problems are necessarily less prevalent within black communities. It might be that drug services are viewed by black people as less accessible and potentially unhelpful. Given the predominant character of Britain's drug problem, the established tradition of drug agencies is to provide services to white opiate users. Consequently, it is not uncommon for black people to perceive drug agencies as run 'by white people, for white people' (Awiah, Butt and Dorn, 1990 and 1991). Even so, black drug users are certainly not unknown to agencies in the Lewisham area. Approximately one-tenth of all male heroin users known to drug agencies, for example, are black.

Quite apart from the fact that black drug users are under-represented among the clients of drug services, we must also admit that there is a distinct possibility that agency records do not allow us to make strict comparisons between black and white drug users. Where cocaine is concerned, for example, given stereotypes of black drug use – to which drug agencies themselves might be prone because of their comparative lack of familiarity with black clients – it is possible that agency workers were more likely to ask questions about (or record mention of) cocaine use where black people are concerned.

If agency reports are taken at face-value, while black and white drug users are very similar in some respects, they are different in others. The majority of both black and white clients, for example, are heroin users. Black clients, on the other hand, are less likely to be using heroin as their sole drug. On the other hand, black people do seem to be proportionately more likely to be using cocaine – either in combination with heroin, or alone. Indeed, it seemed to be much more common for black clients to be using either cocaine or crack alone. The final difference is that black clients seem much less likely to inject drugs, and there is no reason to believe that this is not a sound inference about styles of black drug use. Although there is a distinct possibility that black people are less likely to view conventional drug agencies as relevant to their needs and therefore to use these services, it is difficult to see why black injectors would be less likely to refer themselves for help than non-injectors.

## BLACK AND BLUE: COCAINE AND CRACK USERS KNOWN TO THE POLICE

In summary, helping agencies identified 161 individuals who were using either cocaine or crack. This amounts to one-quarter of all drug users known to these agencies, four-fifths of whom were known to specialist drug services. Crack was specifically mentioned in approximately one-third of all of these cases. The vast majority of those people using either cocaine or crack (82 per cent) were poly-drug users for whom the main drug used was heroin. In terms of the ethnic coding employed in the survey, 80 per cent of cocaine and crack users known to helping agencies were white.

This profile of cocaine and crack users known to helping agencies stands in sharp contrast to police arrests in the Lewisham area for offences related to cocaine or crack. In all cocaine or crack were mentioned in 61 cases of arrest for drug offences, either as the primary offences or as a subsidiary charge – for example, where the charge might have been supply of cannabis, together with the possession of cocaine. In the majority of these cases, however, offences concerned with cocaine or crack were the primary charge. Not all of these persons arrested for cocaine or crack offences were resident in the Lewisham area, and those not resident in Lewisham had been excluded from analysis in the Drug Information Project report. Here, all cocaine and crack arrests are included.

Of these 61 cases, 39 involved black people (of whom 9 were women) and 13 cases involved white men. In nine cases, all men, no ethnic code was supplied. Therefore, in those cases where identification was possible, 75 per cent of arrests for cocaine or crack offences involved black people. This stands in contrast to those cocaine and crack users known to helping agencies, where 80 per cent were white people. Where specific crack offences are concerned, whereas 95 per cent of arrests involved black people, 85 per cent of crack users known to helping agencies were white. One further comparison is that in those cases where the nature of the drug offence was specified (n = 33) black people seemed much more likely to have been charged with supply or intent to supply crack or cocaine, in that 75 per cent of dealing charges ('supply' or 'possession with intent to supply') involved black people.

These areas of disagreement between the profile of cocaine and crack users known to helping agencies, as against those known to the police, reflect a general tendency for different drugs (and different kinds of drug users) to make a radically different impact on the routine workloads of various agencies (see Table 5.4). So that whereas it is heroin misuse which is the major preoccupation for specialist drug agencies, accounting for 85–90 per cent of agency caseloads, only 5 per cent of police arrests involve heroin. By contrast, whereas 80 per cent of police arrests involve cannabis offences (mainly unlawful possession) this is an insignificant part of the workloads of drug agencies, even though a substantial proportion of the clients of drug agencies are known to be cannabis users.

What do these sometimes quite extraordinary multi-agency variations signify? On a hasty reading they might seem to offer no-nonsense evidence of racial discrimination by the police, which has already been demonstrated on many occasions. Perhaps the most celebrated of these is the Policy Studies Institute report on *Police and People in London* which had been commissioned by the Metropolitan

*Table* 5.4    Multi-agency variations in profiles of known drug users
(all percentages rounded to 5 per cent)

|  | Main drug used | | | % Male | % Black |
| | *Heroin* | *Cocaine* | *Cannabis* | | |
| --- | --- | --- | --- | --- | --- |
| Drug agencies | 85 | 5 | – | 65 | 5 |
| Probation | 70 | 10 | 15 | 80 | 20 |
| Social Services | 30 | 5 | 40 | 50 | 20 |
| Police | 5 | 10 | 80 | 90 | 50 |

|  | All drugs used | | | |
| | *Heroin* | *Cocaine* | *Crack* | *Cannabis* |
| --- | --- | --- | --- | --- |
| Drug agencies | 90 | 20 | 10 | 60 |
| Probation | 70 | 25 | – | 50 |
| Social Services | 30 | 10 | 20 | 65 |
| Police | 5 | 10 | 5 | 80 |

Police Commissioner (Smith and Gray, 1985). This was the response
by some sections of the press to the Lewisham survey, exemplified by
the headline in *The Independent* (24 February 1991): 'Drugs Police
"Target Blacks"'.

However, the findings of the DIP survey require a more nuanced
reading. The first thing to notice is that there are two kinds of policing
bundled up together in the police returns contained within the survey. The first is a drugs-specific enforcement strategy which relies
upon intelligence work and surveillance, and which involves targeted
operations against known and suspected dealers and identified locations for drug-dealing. For example, following the first major drug
operation on the Milton Court Estate ('Crack City'), two further
raids were conducted in Deptford which resulted in cocaine and crack
seizures. The first of these, on the Winslade estate, followed complaints from local residents; 15 people were arrested of whom 14 were
black. In the next raid on the Evelyn estate, there were 12 arrests, all
of whom were black people. Police operations such as these undoubtedly only scratch the surface of the drug problem, and are no more
reliable as indications of the drug problem in its totality than the
records of helping agencies. It is even possible that they merely have
the effect of pushing drug-dealing around from one location to
another (Moore, 1977; Manning, 1980; Pearson, 1992). Even so,
when acting on the basis of complaints by neighbours or long-term
surveillance of a particular drug-dealing network, police raids offer

tangible evidence of the specific nature of local drug-dealing. To put the matter bluntly, in drug-enforcement operations of this kind one can hardly blame the police for finding what they found. 'We haven't targeted a community,' said the divisional chief superintendent at a meeting of the local Police Consultative Group, 'but a commodity'.

A quite separate form of policing is involved where the majority of cannabis arrests are concerned, of which more than 90 per cent out of a total of 307 were reported by the local police divisions rather than specialist squads. Arrests for the unlawful possession of cannabis are thus often the result of routine stop-and-search measures by police officers from the uniformed branch, rather than by the CID or the area drug squad. Of the 175 arrests involving cannabis, where a racial coding was supplied, the vast bulk of which came from the police division in the northern part of Lewisham, 44 per cent involved black people. In twelve of these cases, the charge was possession with intent to supply, of whom eleven were black. In 22 drug squad arrests for cannabis offences, by comparison, a lower proportion of 32 per cent involved black people and 25 per cent of supply charges (n = 12) concerned black offenders.

There is abundant evidence from previous research of the discriminatory nature of stop-and-search tactics, exemplified by the workings of the antiquated 'Sus' law which derived from the 1824 Vagrancy Act (Home Affairs Committee, 1980; Willis, 1985; Pearson *et al.*, 1989). In spite of the codes of practice resulting from the 1984 Police and Criminal Evidence Act which require 'reasonable grounds for suspicion' before conducting a search, the 1988 British Crime Survey indicates that young males aged 16–24 are stopped much more frequently than other groups and that the likelihood was even higher for Afro-Caribbeans (Home Office, 1985; Skogan, 1990; Crisp, 1990). Drug arrests resulting from stop-and-search, unlike specialist drug enforcement operations, are not informed by any kind of 'intelligence', other than the routine wisdom of the police 'canteen culture' that black youths are fair game and that 'stop' will often provide a 'result' in the form of a 'spliff' (cf. Smith and Gray, 1985, pp. 405–6). Quite frankly, if one were to go looking for evidence of discriminatory practices, then the profile of cannabis arrests from routine stop-and-search policing would offer a better avenue of enquiry than cocaine offences.

It would still remain necessary, however, to account for the large discrepancy between police arrest statistics and agency records with regard to cocaine and crack whereby 75 per cent of arrests for cocaine and crack offences involved black people whereas 80 per cent of cocaine and crack users known to helping agencies are white? The police view (as stated on more than one occasion by the divisional chief superintendent) was that this was an accurate reflection of the cocaine–crack scene in south London: most of the dealers were black, and most of the users were white.

How are we to judge such a response? It is possible that it is true. A survey technique such as ours can provide no evidence on which to judge the matter, one way or another. Indeed, given the hidden and unknown dimensions of both drug use and drug dealing, there is no basis on which to make a final judgement: the question is simply 'unknowable'. Nevertheless, it is worth noting that it is a viewpoint which would be supported by some (but not all) of those people employed in drug agencies and who possess a detailed working knowledge of the local drug scene. We also know, both from Britain and North America, that people from poor communities and minor-ity ethnic groups who suffer from discrimination in formal labour markets have traditionally employed their entrepreneurial skills in the provision of illicit goods and services – principally, in terms of illegal gambling, prostitution and other aspects of the informal 'twi-light' economy (Reuter, MacCoun and Murphy, 1990; Dench, 1991; Samuels, 1981; Joselit, 1983; Dixon, 1991). In New York, for example, successive instances of immigration – Jewish, Italian, African-American and Hispanic – ripple across the twentieth-century history of the narcotic trade (Courtwright, Joseph and Des Jarlais, 1989). The positioning of disadvantaged and disenfranchised com-munities (both black and white) within the contemporary drug scene continues this tradition whereby for poor communities drugs are both a scourge and an economic generator (Johnson *et al.*, 1985; Williams, 1989; Williams and Kornblum, 1985; Bourgois, 1989; Reuter, Mac-Coun and Murphy, 1990; Gilman and Pearson, 1991). It is therefore hardly a matter for surprise if some black people have attempted to carve out a niche in potentially lucrative low-level drug dealing networks in Britain.

What is unquestionably true, amidst so much confusion of detail and speculation which harbours vast potential for press sensational-ism and misunderstanding, is that for some time the Metropolitan Police, on the basis of intelligence and surveillance operations, have placed considerable emphasis on the role of Afro-Caribbean net-works within London's cocaine–crack distribution system. In evi-dence to the Home Affairs Committee in 1989, the Metropolitan

Police offered a somewhat flamboyant statement that 'at the moment, "crack" is almost exclusively in the province of the black, mostly Jamaican, areas':

> This Force has also identified links between Jamaican organised criminals, 'the so-called Yardies', and drug trafficking. . . . Their common factors are the ethnic origins of those involved and the use of drugs. These individuals are primarily concerned with the pro-duction and distribution of crack and cocaine in inner city areas where policing is already difficult. Many of those involved are Jamaican illegal immigrants who have no fixed addresses but who are bound by their Jamaican origin and reggae culture and who travel from one location to another with regularity. Such is their nomadic lifestyle that serious offences, for example, murders have been, and will continue to be committed wherever the cultural bandwagon happens to stop' (Home Affairs Committee, 1989, pp. 47, 51).

Any properly formulated response to a statement such as this must, by necessity, be multi-faceted. On the one hand, it is one of the undeniable tragedies of the Caribbean region that some of its islands have become established as entrepôts between Latin American coca-growing producer nations and the USA, so that the possibilities of a diversification of cocaine-trafficking along the well-trodden paths of human migration, settlement and commerce between the Caribbean and the British Isles are very real. It is in the geo-political actualities of the Caribbean region that one finds the objective basis for a significant black presence within Britain's cocaine trade.

But in the phrasing of this statement from the Metropolitan Police one finds such a grotesque stereotype, offering a fearful combination of the most explosive cultural images – inner-city violence orches-trated by a black 'mafia' of rootless, drug-dealing, nomadic illegal immigrants – that even the more sensationalist faction of our tabloid newspaper industry might have been judged to have over-reached itself if it had dished up such a lurid picture of inner-city depravity.

## MULTI-AGENCY WORK: A NECESSARY OBJECTIVE, BUT A DIFFICULT ONE

Between these two poles of a possible response, there lies a more immediately answerable and worrying question. A great deal of emphasis has been placed in recent years on improved inter-agency cooperation within the criminal justice system. While this includes the sphere of drug misuse (Pearson, Gilman and McIver, 1986; Metropolitan Police, 1986), it involves a set of arguments which embrace such diverse matters as child abuse, local crime prevention initiatives, including the design and management of housing estates, juvenile offender liaison schemes, community policing, custody diversion, the response to racial attacks, more generalised systems of victim support, neighbourhood watch, and much more (Home Office, 1984; Blagg *et al.*, 1988; Sampson *et al.*, 1988; Pearson *et al.*, 1989 and 1992).

Where drug misuse is concerned, multi-agency work can be expected to have its most significant impact at the interface between helping agencies and the criminal justice system. The probation service is, of course, often a crucial pivot at this interface: particularly where attempts to divert offenders from custody are concerned. Recent proposals from the Home Office (1988 and 1990) have suggested ways of strengthening the effort to divert offenders from custody under the not-always-helpful rubric of 'punishment in the community'. These proposals nevertheless have much to commend them where offenders with drug-related problems are concerned. They can offer a means to channel drug users and less serious offenders such as user–dealers towards helping agencies, thus encouraging them to take 'early retirement' from their drug-using careers (Gilman and Pearson, 1991). It is also by means such as these that 'harm reduction' principles might be extended into the criminal justice system (Pearson, 1992). Considerations such as these are given added urgency by the advent of HIV and AIDS, together with increasing evidence of both the availability of drugs in British prisons and dangerously high levels of high-risk activities such as sharing injecting equipment and unsafe sex practices among male prisoners (ACMD, 1988 and 1989; Rahman, Ditton and Forsyth, 1989; Carvell and Hart, 1990; Kennedy *et al.*, 1990).

Although many of the recommendations of the Advisory Council on the Misuse of Drugs concerning HIV and AIDS are framed with heroin users in mind, cocaine users are not exempt from these considerations. And certainly not when, in the case of the Lewisham survey, approximately two-thirds of all cocaine users are injecting poly-drug users and one-third are known to be injecting cocaine. People who inject cocaine are more likely to inject more frequently during the day than opiate users, and thereby to increase the likelihood of being forgetful or making a 'mistake' in terms of safe injection practices. Cocaine is also widely recognised as a sexual stimulant which even when inhaled, or smoked in its freebase form ('crack'), will reduce levels of risk-perception and the avoidance of high-risk sex practices. The application of the Advisory Committee's recommendations to cocaine misuse, and to less serious offenders such as user–dealers of cocaine or crack, is therefore a matter which could be most usefully addressed.

Multi-agency initiatives are invariably difficult to manage and sustain because of inherent conflicts between different agencies in the state and voluntary sector (Blagg *et al.*, 1988; Sampson *et al.*, 1988 and 1991; Pearson *et al.*, 1992). One aspect of these conflicts is the uneven traffic of power-differentials which run between different agencies: quite simply, some agencies are more powerful than others. Without questioning the need for an effective law-enforcement strategy to counter the threat of drug misuse, it remains true that the police service in Britain is a powerful and articulate force. As a consequence, in multi-agency forums the police voice invariably carries the day (Sampson *et al.*, 1988).

More generally, in public discourse and news values, the police view on social issues is often dominant. Where cocaine use in Britain is concerned, it would be a tragedy if the police view – which so often seems to portray a black 'dope-fiend' set loose in our midst – defined the agenda, without qualification or opposition. The specific qualification which must be entered into the equation on the basis of the Lewisham survey is that it would be deeply misleading if responses to cocaine misuse were planned on the assumption that cocaine and crack use was predominantly a black phenomenon.

The drugs intelligence of the Metropolitan Police might well be accurate in defining the way in which some black dealers have established an economic niche within the low-level cocaine and crack trade. It nevertheless risks setting in motion a self-fulfilling prophecy whereby black drug users and black communities are targeted for police operations, thereby further criminalising and alienating the black community and obstructing not only the movement towards racial justice but also the quest for an effective drug control policy.

REFERENCES

Advisory Council on the Misuse of Drugs (1988) *AIDS and Drug Misuse, Part I* (London: HMSO).
—— (1989) *AIDS and Drug Misuse, Part II* (London: HMSO).
J. Awiah, S. Butt and N. Dorn (1990) '"The Last Place I Would Go": Black People and Drug Services in Britain', *Druglink*, Vol. 5, no. 5, pp. 14–15.
—— (1992) *Race, Gender and Drug Services*, (London: Institute for the Study of Drug Dependence).
H. Blagg, G. Pearson, A. Sampson, D. Smith and P. Stubbs (1988) 'Inter-Agency Cooperation: Rhetoric and Reality', in T. Hope and M. Shaw (eds), *Communities and Crime Reduction* (London: HMSO).
P. Bourgois (1989) 'Crack in Spanish Harlem: Culture and Economy in the Inner City', *Anthropology Today*, Vol. 5, no. 4, pp. 6–11.
A. Burr (1987) 'Chasing the Dragon: Heroin Misuse, Delinquency and Crime in the Context of South London Culture', *British Journal of Criminology*, Vol. 27, no. 4, pp. 333–57.
—— (1989) 'An Inner-City Community Response to Heroin Use', in S. MacGregor (ed.), *Drugs and British Society* (London: Routledge).
A. L. M. Carvell and G. J. Hart (1990) 'Risk Behaviours for HIV Infection among Drug Users in Prison', *British Medical Journal*, Vol. 300, 26 May 1990, pp. 1383–4.
D. Courtwright, H. Joseph and D. Des Jarlais (1989) *Addicts Who Survived: An oral history of narcotic users in America, 1912–1965* (Tennessee: University of Tennessee Press).
D. Crisp (1990) 'The Police and the Public', *Home Office Research Bulletin*, no. 29, pp. 15–17.
G. Dench (1991) *Crime in a Minority Situation: The Maltese Case* (London: Institute of Community Studies).
Department of Health (1990) *Data from the Addicts Index, January to December 1989* (London: DOH).
D. Dixon (1991) *From Prohibition to Regulation: Bookmaking, Anti-Gambling and the Law* (Oxford: Oxford University Press).
N. Dorn and N. South (eds) (1987) *A Land Fit for Heroin? Drug Policies, Prevention and Practice* (London: Macmillan).
C. Fazey, P. Brown and P. Batey (1990) *A Socio-Demographic Analysis of Patients Attending a Drug Dependency Clinic* (Liverpool: Centre for Urban Studies, University of Liverpool).
J. Giggs, P. Bean, D. Whynes and C. Wilkinson (1989) 'Class-A Drug Users: Prevalence and Characteristics in Greater Nottingham', *British Journal of Addiction*, Vol. 84, pp. 1473–80.
M. Gilman and G. Pearson (1991) 'Lifestyles and Law Enforcement' in P. Bean and D. K. Whynes (eds), *Policing and Prescribing: The British System of Drug Control* (London: Macmillan).
M. Gilman, P. Traynor and G. Pearson (1990) 'The Limits of Intervention: Cyclizine Misuse', *Druglink*, Vol. 5, no. 3, pp. 12–13.
R. Hartnoll, R. Lewis, M. Mitcheson and S. Bryer (1985a) 'Estimating the Prevalence of Opioid Dependence', *The Lancet*, 26 January 1985, pp. 203–5.

R. Hartnoll, E. Daviaud, R. Lewis and M. Mitcheson (1985b) *Drug Problems: Assessing Local Needs* (London: Drug Indicators Project, Birkbeck College, University of London).

S. Haw (1985) *Drug Problems in Greater Glasgow* (London: SCODA).

Home Affairs Committee (1980) *Race Relations and the 'Sus' Law*, Second Report from the Home Affairs Committee, Session 1979–80, HC 559 (London: HMSO).

—— (1989) *Drug Trafficking and Related Serious Crime, Vol. II: Minutes of Evidence and Appendices*, HC 370–II (London: HMSO).

Home Office (1984) *Crime Prevention*, Home Office Circular HO 8/84.

—— (1985) *Police and Criminal Evidence Act 1984 (s. 66) Codes of Practice* (London: HMSO).

—— (1988) *Punishment, Custody and the Community*, Cm. 424, (London: HMSO).

—— (1990) *Crime, Justice and Protecting the Public: The Government's Proposals for Legislation*, Cm. 965 (London: HMSO).

S. Hyde, S. Balloch and P. Ainley (1989) *A Social Atlas of Poverty in Lewisham* (London: Centre for Inner City Studies, Goldsmiths' College, University of London).

Inner London Probation Service (1990) *Drug and Alcohol Misuse: Summary of Demonstration Unit Interviews* (London: ILPS).

B. O. Johnson, P. L. Goldstein, E. Preble, J. Schmeidler, D. J. Lipton, B. Spunt and T. Miller (1985) *Taking Care of Business: The Economics of Crime by Heroin Abusers* (Lexington, Mass.: Lexington Books).

J. W. Joselit (1983) *Our Gang: Jewish Crime and the New York Jewish Community, 1900–1940* (Bloomington: Indiana University Press).

D. Kennedy, G. Mair, L. Elliot and J. Ditton (1990) *Illicit Drug Use, Injecting and Syringe Sharing in Scottish Prisons in the 1990s* (Glasgow: START (Substance Treatment Agency Reporting Team), University of Glasgow).

D. Laister and G. Pearson (1988) *Hammersmith and Fulham Drug and Alcohol Survey: Final Report* (London: London Borough of Hammersmith and Fulham).

C. Lightbrown (1990) *Millwall in the Community* (London: Millwall Football Club).

P. K. Manning (1980) *The Narcs' Game: Organisational and Informational Limits on Drug Law Enforcement* (Cambridge, Mass.: MIT Press).

Metropolitan Police (1986) *Drug Abuse: A Guide for Divisions on the Formation of Multi-Agency Cooperation* (London: New Scotland Yard).

H. S. Mirza, G. Pearson and S. Phillips (1991) *Drugs, People and Services in Lewisham: Final Report of the Drug Information Project* (London: Goldsmiths' College, University of London).

M. H. Moore (1977) *Buy and Bust: The Effective Regulation of an Illicit Market in Heroin* (Lexington, Mass.: Lexington Books).

H. Parker, K. Bakx and R. Newcombe (1988) *Living with Heroin: The Impact of a Drugs 'Epidemic' on an English Community* (Milton Keynes: Open University Press).

C. J. Pattison, E. A. Barnes and A. Thorley (1982) *South Tyneside Drug Prevalence and Indicators Survey* (Newcastle-upon-Tyne: Centre for

Alcohol and Drug Studies, St Nicholas Hospital, Newcastle-upon-Tyne).

G. Pearson (1987a) *The New Heroin Users* (Oxford: Basil Blackwell).

—— (1987b) 'Social Deprivation, Unemployment and Patterns of Heroin Use', in N. Dorn and N. South (eds), *A Land Fit for Heroin? Drug Policies, Prevention and Practice* (London: Macmillan).

—— (1991a) 'British Drug Control Policies', in M. Tonry (ed.), *Crime and Justice: A Review*, Vol. 14 (Chicago: University of Chicago Press).

—— (1991b) 'Drug Problems and Social Work', in P. Carter, T. Jeffs and M. K. Smith (eds), *Social Work and Social Welfare Yearbook 3* (Milton Keynes: Open University Press).

—— (1992) 'Drugs and Criminal Justice: A Harm Reduction Perspective', in P. O'Hare, R. Newcombe, A. Matthews, E. Buning and E. Drucker (eds), *The Reduction of Drug-Related Harm* (London: Routledge).

G. Pearson and M. Gilman (1992) 'Local and Regional Variations in Drug Misuse', in J. Strang and M. Gossop (eds), *Responding to Drug Misuse: The British System* (Oxford: Oxford University Press, in press).

G. Pearson, M. Gilman and S. McIver (1985) 'Heroin Use in the North of England', *Health Education Journal*, Vol. 45, no. 3, pp. 186–9.

—— (1986) *Young People and Heroin: An Examination of Heroin Use in the North of England* (London: Health Education Council [2nd edition, 1987, Aldershot: Gower]).

G. Pearson, A. Sampson, H. Blagg, P. Stubbs and D. Smith (1989), 'Policing Racism', in R. Morgan and D. J. Smith (eds), *Coming to Terms with Policing: Perspectives on Policy* (London: Routledge).

G. Pearson, H. Blagg, D. Smith, A. Sampson and P. Stubbs (1992) 'Crime, Community and Conflict: The Multi-Agency Approach', in D. Downes (ed.), *Unravelling Criminal Justice: Eleven Case Studies* (London: Macmillan).

M. Z. Rahman, J. Ditton and A. J. M. Forsyth (1989) 'Variations in Needle Sharing Practices Among Intravenous Drug Users in Possil (Glasgow)', *British Journal of Addiction*, Vol. 84, pp. 923–7.

P. Reuter, R. MacCoun and P. Murphy (1990) *Money from Crime: A Study of the Economics of Drug Dealing in Washington, D.C.* (Santa Monica, California: RAND Corporation).

W. S. Robinson (1950) 'Ecological Correlations and the Behaviour of Individuals', *American Sociological Review*, Vol. 15, pp. 351–7.

Safe Neighbourhoods Unit (1990) *The Milton Court Report* (London: Safe Neighbourhoods Unit and Lewisham Safer Cities Project).

R. Samuels (1981) *East End Underworld: Chapters in the Life of Arthur Harding* (London: Routledge and Kegan Paul).

A. Sampson, P. Stubbs, D. Smith, G. Pearson and H. Blagg (1988) 'Crime, Localities and the Multi-Agency Approach', *British Journal of Criminology*, Vol. 28, no. 4, pp. 478–93.

A. Sampson, D. Smith, G. Pearson, H. Blagg and P. Stubbs (1991) 'Gender Issues in Inter-Agency Relations: Police, Probation and Social Services', in P. Abbott and C. Wallace (eds), *Gender, Power and Sexuality* (London: Macmillan).

W. G. Skogan (1990) *The Police and Public in England and Wales: A British*

*Crime Survey Report*, Home Office Research Study no. 117 (London: HMSO).

D. J. Smith and S. Gray (1985) *Police and People in London: The PSI Report* (Aldershot: Gower).

Southwark Drug Misuse Consultative Group (1989) *Smoking Cocaine in Southwark* (London: mimeo).

G. V. Stimson and E. Oppenheimer (1982) *Heroin Addiction: Treatment and Control in Britain* (London: Tavistock).

J. Strang, P. Griffiths and M. Gossop (1990) 'Crack and Cocaine Use in South London Drug Addicts: 1987–1989', *British Journal of Addiction*, Vol. 85, pp. 193–6.

S. Tippell and F. Aston (1990) *Cocaine Use: The US Experience and the Implications for Drug Services in Britain* (London: Community Drug Project).

P. Townsend (1987) *Poverty and Labour in London* (London: Low Pay Unit).

T. Williams (1989) *The Cocaine Kids* (New York: Addison-Wesley).

T. Williams and W. Kornblum (1985) *Growing Up Poor* (Lexington, Mass.: Lexington Books).

C. F. Willis (1985) 'The Use, Effectiveness and Impact of Police Stop and Search Powers', in K. Heal, R. Tarling and J. Burrows (eds), *Policing Today* (London: HMSO).

# 6 Civil Rights and Civil Liberties surrounding the use of Cocaine and Crack

Jane Goodsir

## INTRODUCTION

In the early 1980s the UK became engaged in a war on drugs. During the later part of the decade, the battle focused on cocaine. Some of the developments that emerged as part of the war strategy have directly threatened the civil liberties of the general public, as well as cocaine users and dealers.

Rights and civil liberties in the UK have been described as a state of mind, rather than a set of rules, relying on institutions and formal procedures, rather than a charter or written constitution.[1] There is no overriding principle from which 'rights' are derived. Instead, we have to look at a web of different legal cases, Home Office guidelines, and official procedures to determine what freedoms we enjoy as citizens.

The policing of drug users, in the widest sense of the term, is always controversial, as it is concerned with the control of individual choice – to take drugs, or not. The legal distribution of drugs like cocaine has during this century been delegated to the medical profession and pharmacists, who are expected to exert a high degree of care and control. Other drugs, like alcohol, form a traditional part of our culture and are available with relatively few legal controls. Different societies choose to control different types of individual drug use.

In the UK, control of cocaine use has taken place alongside the control of other drugs. Isolating civil liberties issues surrounding cocaine use would be difficult, if not impossible. This chapter will therefore look at civil liberties issues surrounding illegal drug use in general, as well as dealing with specific cocaine-related developments.

While the battle against crack–cocaine has taken on particularly British dimensions, nevertheless comparisons with the US are relevant. There, the war on crack has been characterised as a war on black ghetto youth – a means of mobilising opinion against poorer

130

people who are not covered by health and other insurance, and who are not part of mainstream society.[2] In the UK, where different social institutions and traditions of intervention and public service provision have been maintained, the war on cocaine and crack has been considerably more muted.[3]

There have been significant shifts in relation to civil liberties over the past ten years. Illegal drug use, and fear of the consequences of that use, have been used as a justification for a variety of measures in what has been seen as a crisis. However, the erosion of individual rights during the period is complex, with many interweaving strands. It would be fair to say that the apparent emergency presented by drug trafficking, and particularly fear of cocaine trafficking, has enabled politicians to introduce quite intrusive measures directed specifically at drug users and traffickers, with relatively little public debate or opposition. In this respect, there are parallels between the UK and the US. Some legislation has been inspired by US and Reaganite concerns, while other legislation has a particularly British background.

By no means all developments threatening individual freedoms have occurred as a direct result of government legislation. For example, increased drug monitoring of different sections of the population is associated with changing professional attitudes and networks, information about drugs, cheap testing procedures, and new approaches to personnel management. But before looking at civil rights and liberties in detail, it may be useful to review recent perceptions of the drugs problem.

During the early 1980s, the issue of illegal drug use in the UK gave rise to political concern that had been dormant since the 1960s. Illegal drugs and the management of drug problems became a matter of general interest. In the US, Ronald and Nancy Reagan took up the issue, campaigning vigorously to eradicate drug misuse. In the UK, politicians were tempted to follow the US approach, where drug problems among the urban poor had long been established. But over the years, different traditions of treatment had developed in the UK and indeed, in Europe, reflecting prevailing cultural and public health service values.[4] A battle was fought between politicians and other groups concerned with the delivery of health and other services to illegal drug users.[5]

The US approach focused on the perceived threat of crack–cocaine can perhaps be seen as blaming and otherwise isolating drug users. For example,

The . . number of reported child abuse cases in New York City has
gone in 1986 from 2,200 reported cases to 1988, 8,000 cases (sic). It
has gone up by 400%, almost all of them the children of Cocaine/
Crack using parents. . . . Of all the kids who died by battering in
New York City, 73% were the children of Crack/Cocaine using
parents.'[6]

This sensational 1989 speech by Robert Stutman of the US Drug
Enforcement Agency described the horrors of the drug 'crack' to a
group of senior British police officers. The speech received wide
publicity. In the US, where politicians originated the 'War on Drugs',
social work professionals were at the forefront of what has been
called a 'harm maximisation programme' through 'user accountability'.[7] For example, pregnant women have been subject to criminal prosecutions for neglect of the foetus,

usually triggered by a hospital's report of a positive toxicology to a
state agency. This practice violates both the woman's right to
nondisclosure of private information and the physician's ethical
obligation to protect doctor–patient confidentiality.[8]

While drug users in the UK have not become subject to such
prosecutions, disclosure of a drugs problem in the criminal courts can
still cause great difficulty, and may be greeted with ignorance and
intolerance. It may be grossly prejudicial to the outcome of a case.
Women, in particular, may be seen by sentencers as 'unfeminine' and
defiant of conventional morality. As addicts they are at risk of being
punished for both the offence, and for their failure to be 'good' wives
and mothers.

While there has been pressure to follow the US approach to drug
'user accountability', the British approach has differed significantly,
as an alliance of professionals fought for greater freedom for staff at
street-level to make contact with users and to provide 'harm reduction' programmes.

Changes in UK drug policy took place through the 1980s in response to rising levels of drug use, and later, to evidence of strong
links between injecting drug use involving shared needles, and HIV
infection. While the extent of UK illegal drug use is unknown,
different statistics provide a series of indicators about possible trends
in drug use. In 1989, over 38 000 people were dealt with (either
convicted or cautioned) for drugs offences. Most were cannabis users
under 30. A sharp rise in the numbers of people convicted for heroin

offences occurred in the mid 1980s, and in 1989 there was a sharp rise in the numbers convicted of cocaine offences.

While such statistics reflect levels of police activity to some extent, figures on addicts notified to the Home Office as receiving drugs treatment also show a marked increase, from under 2000 in 1979, to nearly 15 000 in 1989. Of these, the overwhelming majority (87 per cent) were notified as addicted to heroin in 1989. Only a very small minority were actively seeking treatment in relation to cocaine dependence. Nevertheless, it was perceived that there was a cocaine problem, even if it was unreported through drug treatment statistics.

From the mid-1980s onwards, speculation from different authorities on cocaine use was reported frequently by the British press. There were a number of elements of concern – who was using, and were users likely to develop behaviour patterns similar to their allegedly depraved US counterparts? Above all, who was making the money? Policymakers showed an inclination to respond to perceived threats posed by Columbian cocaine barons, and 'Yardies', Jamaican/American drug dealing syndicates associated with violent crime in US cities like New York.

While social institutions, culture, and patterns of drug taking in the UK have differed markedly from those in the US, British policymakers adopted some measures similar to those taken in the US 'War on Drugs'. Measures taken in the US have been said to amount to an erosion of civil liberties. The imperative of drugs enforcement has led to an attack on government protections of individual rights. At the same time, there has been a gradual rise of 'big brotherism', in which possible drug takers (and ordinary citizens) are subject to monitoring, surveillance and other intrusive actions.[9] Similar measures have been proposed, if not always introduced, in the UK.

In looking at the British response to crack–cocaine and civil liberties, it may be helpful to explore some basic individual freedoms: the question of personal liberty and police powers, sentencing and fair trial, the right to privacy and confidentiality in the provision of personal services, freedom from undue control, and freedom from discrimination. But before we look at these basic freedoms, it is important to understand the significance of the Drug Trafficking Offences Act 1986 and its far-reaching effect on civil liberties.

## THE DRUG TRAFFICKING OFFENCES ACT, 1986

The Drug Trafficking Offences Act, 1986 (DTOA) is a direct attack on profiteering by drug dealers. Enacted in what was perceived to be a crisis, in which cocaine barons were turning over millions in profits and laundering profits through 'respectable' channels, the legislation was intended to incorporate elements of criminal law and sentencing, law of receivership, and common law injunctions freezing suspected proceeds of crime. In 1984, the Hodgson Committee had already recommended increasing the effectiveness of forfeiture orders where there was *prima facie* evidence that indictable offences had been committed. As public attitudes were seen to harden against drug pushers, the DTOA was passed with relatively little opposition, although it raised some fundamental questions about general freedom and the right to privacy.

The DTOA is unusual, as it gives immunity from civil or criminal liability to those disclosing suspicions concerning the proceeds of drug trafficking. It also makes it an offence for anyone aware of an investigation to tip off the suspect. Police involved in investigating drug trafficking offences may compel those providing, for example, financial services to breach confidentiality. They may search for and seize material held by parties not suspected of crime. Police may apply to court for orders freezing and confiscating suspect assets acquired up to six years previously. The freezing of assets may be carried out before charges have been laid. It reverses the burden of proof in relation to suspect property, following conviction for a trafficking offence.[10]

People not involved in crime who unsuspectingly take possession of property being the proceeds of drug trafficking can also find themselves subject to confiscation orders under the Act. For example, the daughter of a drug trafficker who was given a car as a present from drug-trafficking proceeds would lose the car, even if she had no reason to suspect the car was bought with 'tainted' money. The wife of a suspected drug trafficker with her own legitimate personal income might find her bank account frozen during the course of proceedings under the Act, and might need to account in great detail for her personal income and expenditure in order to retain her legitimate savings and other property.

Judges have commented on this 'striking and extraordinary consequence of the 1986 Act . . . the court's powers (were) so draconian that it seemed to be able to deprive the legal owner of some or all of his or her beneficial interest in (the property) without the owner having any opportunity to present the arguments against such a conclusion'.

## PERSONAL LIBERTY AND GENERAL POLICE POWERS

Over the years, much conflict has arisen over aspects of drugs policing. Police powers to stop and search were greatly enhanced by the Misuse of Drugs Act 1971, when police were given the power to detain in order to conduct a drugs search. By the early 1980s a number of riots and public order incidents had occurred as a result of injudicious use of stop and search powers in inner-city areas (Bristol, Brixton and so on). While these urban riots involved both black and white youth, they were often associated with drugs policing. Drugs, policing and issues of race had in the minds of many people become interconnected, with an adverse effect on public confidence and cooperation.

## INCREASED POWERS OF SEARCH

By 1986, the Police and Criminal Evidence Act (PACE) introduced more comprehensive police powers to search individuals, and to set up road blocks to search vehicles in areas where there was a pattern of serious crime in an area – such as drug dealing. In a climate where public cooperation and confidence in the police was declining, for the first time police were empowered to conduct searches of premises where the occupiers were *not* suspected of crime. (PACE, Drug Trafficking Offences Act 1986 s27 (1)). In addition, new powers were introduced, enabling the police to cause intimate body searches to be made of those suspected of serious offences – such as supply of cocaine.

A number of mass searches of individuals and premises under the new PACE powers relating to cocaine were conducted in 'front-line' areas during the mid 1980s in notorious incidents such as those at Broadwater Farm and in Brixton. Police believed that black 'Yardie' gangs from New York and Jamaica had taken control of some public housing estates and were introducing cocaine, and later 'crack' to the young urban poor. While police said that local communities were being terrorised by a new breed of violent cocaine dealers, and had sought help, these assertions were sometimes disputed by local residents after police operations had been carried out.

## INCREASED CONTROL OF ACCESS TO LEGAL ADVICE

One important police power relating to detention and investigation of offences is the control of access to legal advice. Before PACE, the legal position on rights of access was relatively unclear. After PACE, police gained a new power to defer access to legal assistance for up to 36 hours when investigating serious offences such as drug trafficking. This power affects the capacity of the detainee to exercise the right to silence, a significant individual liberty. In offences involving possession of illegal drugs with intent to supply (trafficking offences), admissions by detainees to the police often have great evidential value. Indeed such self-incrimination often constitutes the only evidence of trafficking, as opposed to possession of drugs.

Many drug users make statements admitting more serious offences after spending considerable periods in police custody, experiencing the pressures of both detention and withdrawal from drugs. Of course, police custody officers are obliged to call in medical help if drug problems are disclosed, but police surgeons seldom prescribe medication along the lines customarily employed by doctors working in drug dependency units. Indeed, drug users who are merely witnesses, rather than suspects of serious crime, can find themselves in detention and under pressure, making witness statements that they subsequently regret.

Special powers for investigating drugs offences were inserted into PACE under the Drug Trafficking Offences Act 1986, allowing police to delay informing relatives and access to lawyers if there are grounds for believing that recovery of a suspect's trafficking proceeds will be hindered.

## EROSION OF THE RIGHT TO SILENCE

In 1988, government proposed to abolish the right to silence, making a major alteration to the 'presumption of innocence'. It was said that major criminals were getting away with crime because they knew how to 'operate the system'. By keeping quiet, and refusing to answer questions, detainees are able to avoid self-incrimination, and the focus of police investigations and subsequent prosecutions become objective evidence, rather than errors made by a defendant while disorientated.

It was proposed that the present caution – a warning administered in theory to all detainees before interview, reminding them of the right to silence – would be abolished. Adverse conclusions were to be drawn about the guilt of defendants who had refused to answer police questions. In drug trafficking cases, particularly those involving relatively small quantities of drugs, police interviews with arrested people tend to be a focal point in contested trials. However, a committee set up with the responsibility of coming up with practical proposals for abolition failed to report publicly, and the matter seems to have lapsed for the present.

Maintaining silence is relatively difficult if an arrested person stands to lose substantial amounts of property in addition to being charged with an offence. The Drug Trafficking Offences Act, 1986, allows the police to investigate, freeze and recover proceeds of drug trafficking. Interviews in relation to proceeds are carried out by drug squad officers to identify property that may be caught by the Act (and to discount property that has been legitimately acquired). The burden of proof is on the defendant to show that property and income has been legitimate. Knowing that his assets, and those of his dependants, may be frozen and forfeit makes it very difficult for an arrested person to resist questioning of this kind.

## NEW POLICE POWERS TO SEIZE PROPERTY

In addition to having powers to seize the property of suspected drug traffickers, together PACE and the DTOA provided for access to and seizure of material and property belonging to others not directly connected with crime. In this way, friends, associates, even professionals providing confidential services, have found themselves forced to disclose information and to give up property and records, as requested by the police. For example, solicitors dealing with confidential conveyancing casework have been compelled by the courts to hand over legally privileged documents under DTOA proceedings.

## SENTENCING AND FAIR TRIAL

**Higher Sentencing**

During the early 1980s a consensus emerged among politicians and the judiciary that drugs sentencing had become too soft. There was a feeling that a comprehensive 'crackdown' on drug suppliers was necessary. In 1983, Lord Lane, C. J. asserted that

> anything which courts of this country can do by way of deterrent sentences on those found guilty of crimes involving Class A drugs should be done.

The case of *R. v. Aramah* was a landmark in English law, as it was the first in a line of cases offering very coherent and persuasive guidelines for sentencers. In *Aramah*, Lord Lane delivered a new sentencing tariff for drugs offences to ensure much more uniform sentencing patterns, reducing the capacity for individual defendants to mitigate their offences. Reduction of sentences from the 'tariff' would only be appropriate where there had been a confession of guilt, coupled with very substantial help to the police.

Minimising the capacity of individual defendants to have their circumstances taken into account may be seen as a loss of liberty, or at least, a formal adjustment of judicial discretion against the individual.

*Aramah* established that appropriate sentences for trafficking of Class A drugs like cocaine would in future be determined by the estimated street-value of the drugs. Courts usually relied on estimates of street prices provided by the police. Sometimes, police valuations of drugs appeared unrealistically high to defendants, depending on complicated 'multiplier' equations with few concessions to relative volatility of street drug prices.[11] Yet such valuations were difficult to challenge, giving the police a degree of influence, albeit indirect, over sentencing patterns.

As a result of *Aramah*, those importing Class-A drugs with a value of over £1 000 000 would receive 12 to 14 years (the maximum), with other adjustments made lower down the sentencing scale. However, by 1985, *Aramah* was already out of date, and Parliament passed the Controlled Drugs (Penalties) Act, increasing maximum sentences to life imprisonment. By 1987, sentences had been adjusted to take account of inflation.

One key problem of deterrent sentencing is that its effectiveness may be questioned. Another problem is undoubtedly that of differentiating between defendants, making an adequate distinction between mere couriers and those actually making the money. This sentencing policy has meant that a large number of relatively insignificant black and other ethnic minority women who acted as cocaine couriers during the late 1980s, have received deterrent prison sentences. Indeed, a very substantial proportion of the female prison population are now serving sentences for drugs offences.

Although all sentences for drug trafficking offences are relatively harsh, until recently those serving higher drug related sentences were additionally subject to the 'Brittan' restrictions on parole, excluding serious drugs offenders from consideration of early release from prison. Effectively, this meant that drugs offenders served longer sentences.

For offenders who are non-UK citizens, facing deportation after serving their sentence, there is an additional problem. Even those eligible for early release have been unlikely to receive supervision following deportation. This has posed a dilemma for those making decisions about parole, and has restricted access to parole in some cases.

## FAIR TRIAL

We have already seen that under the Drug Trafficking Offences Act (DTOA) a number of new measures were introduced that affect a number of traditional 'rights'. The Act has an impact on sentencing. If the total proceeds of trafficking cannot be realised by the prosecution, a period of imprisonment can be imposed in default, running consecutively to any term passed for the original offence. One problem here is the way in which the assessment of proceeds is made. The court can assume that all the defendant's expenditure up to six years before the proceedings began were met out of drug-trafficking proceeds, along with property acquired. Payments and gifts made to innocent third parties may be caught up in the proceedings. In this way, lawyers receiving fees from traffickers for legal representation may be caught by the Act. The onus for proving that income was not derived from trafficking passes to the defendant – who will need to have kept comprehensive records in order to establish legitimate income. Hearsay evidence about expenditure and property is accepted by the courts.

This all serves to isolate the drug trafficker from professional advisers. When applied to defence lawyers, this potential isolation is a matter of some concern, for the ability of a defendant to mount an effective defence and receive a fair trial can be prejudiced.

## PRIVACY AND CONFIDENTIALITY

The monitoring of potential drugs users, dealers and their associates is quite widespread. We have seen that third parties providing professional services to traffickers may become caught up in DTOA proceedings. Bankers, accountants, even solicitors dealing with property transactions, have been approached by the police for confidential information about clients. In disclosing information, these professionals are granted immunity from breach of contract proceedings relating to confidentiality. In one instance, a solicitor's office was searched for documents relating to property transactions undertaken on behalf of a suspected trafficker. In these circumstances the adviser has a duty of confidentiality to the police. If the client were tipped off about the investigation, the adviser could be subject to criminal proceedings under the DTOA.

Concerns about crack–cocaine and other drugs are not restricted to the area of criminal law. As levels of problem drug use rose during the 1980s, increasing numbers of different professionals with statutory responsibilities made contact with drug users, and had to make an appropriate response. Making decisions in relative isolation from one another, these professionals have often been influenced by the prevailing punitive climate.

Some professional staff have overreacted in cases where allegations of illegal drug use have been made. Midwives, community nurses, and even educational welfare officers and teachers have found themselves responding to problems posed by illicit drug users. Those with little drugs casework experience have found it difficult to make an appropriate response.

## MONITORING IN EMPLOYMENT

Ordinary employees are increasingly subject to monitoring for cocaine and other drug use. Doctors may have been seen as the principal professional group coming into contact with drug users.

Doctors working in the field of addiction face a higher level of bureaucratic control than other medical specialists (through monitoring by the Home Office as well as the Department of Health).

Outside the addiction field, doctors are often used by employers to conduct health checks on job applicants. As US-style personnel management techniques were imported to the UK, so health checks including drug tests became relatively common, particularly in service industries. Such drug tests are not necessarily disclosed to job applicants.

While drug-testing has not been introduced for all state-financed employees, as it has in the US, there has been some enthusiasm for testing in private companies. The introduction of drug tests for existing staff as a condition of employment caused a number of minor disputes during the 1980s. One can assume that with the availability of the 'hair' test, relatively non-intrusive from a physical point of view, checks will increase. Such tests, focusing on drug-taking rather than employee performance, may only identify casual cocaine users, rather than employees who have serious substance abuse problems.

## MONITORING OF WOMEN

It has been argued in the US that monitoring of 'crack' mothers too poor to qualify for ante-natal care is a means of diverting attention from the inadequacies of the US health system. Poor mothers are blamed rather than given assistance to deal with their problems. Some have maintained that it is difficult to distinguish between birth complications that arise because of poverty, and those that are attributable to cocaine use.[12] While health facilities are generally more available in the UK than in the US, monitoring of drug-using women, and allegations of foetal abuse, have occurred here.

In 1985, a baby was born to a drug-dependent mother in Berkshire, who had taken drugs in excess of those prescribed by her doctor. The child was detained in hospital until a place-of-safety order was obtained six weeks after the birth under the Children and Young Persons Act, 1969. A series of interim care orders were obtained, and the ensuing legal battle took place over the next 18 months, with widespread publicity. At first, the juvenile panel took the view 'that drug use during pregnancy could itself constitute grounds for a care order under the Act'.[13]

Eventually, in late 1986, the House of Lords found that drug use during pregnancy could be evidence of 'a continuum' of neglect or ill-treatment. By 1987, there was concern that some social services departments had begun automatically to place children of known drug-users on the 'at risk' register.

A compromise was reached when a working party produced a set of guidelines for work with drug-abusing parents, concluding that

> automatic child abuse registration will deter parents from approaching drug dependence units or other professionals for help . . . (and) such a general policy loses sight of the specific needs of a child, which may vary as widely in drug-using as in non-drug-using families.[14]

This initiative signalled the development of specialist drugs training for staff with statutory responsibilities, and an uneasy partnership between drugs service staff and other professionals.

Confidentiality, and the limits to confidentiality, remain points of possible conflict between professionals who come into contact with women using drugs like cocaine.

Misunderstandings between different services providing assistance or supervision to drug users occur quite frequently, depending on the focus of services. Drugs services, concerned with delivery of services to parents, sometimes find themselves in conflict with other services concerned with monitoring and generally providing a range of support to different family members.


## FREEDOM FROM UNDUE CONTROL

### Prisons

The state and state employees exercise power over different groups who may be seen as a threat to themselves or others. While control of ordinary citizens may be insidious, control of prisoners, and those subject to mental health and other orders, is overt.

A large number of people currently imprisoned for drug offences are serving time for cocaine offences, a disproportionate number of whom are black. Despite the difficulties involved in prison over-crowding, drugs offenders do not always qualify for the same remission as other prisoners. This means that time served for a cocaine offence is longer than time served for other offences.

## DRUGS TREATMENT AND INTER-AGENCY COOPERATION

As cocaine users are prosecuted and pass through police stations, or become subject to quasi-judicial decisions by welfare staff with statutory powers, they are dealt with by staff from different agencies whose role may be unclear. Police, social workers, and even staff in drug treatment services are working more closely together than ever before. This 'multi-agency' approach can work in favour of drug users, allowing them help and access to resources that they may never have considered contacting. But becoming subject to a network where negotiation takes place between professionals with different welfare and enforcement responsibilities can bring its ambiguities, and even dangers. If certain social or drugs welfare facilities are threatening or hostile to drug users, there are good reasons for staying away from them.

In the 1988 Home Office paper 'Punishment, Custody and the Community' 1988 (s.3.25), the monitoring of drugs offenders by means of urine tests taken in treatment was recommended. Sentencing reforms aimed at reducing the number of drugs offenders sent to prison may soon include a condition of treatment imposed by the court designed to reduce an offender's dependence on drugs or alcohol. Treatment under order may be accompanied by a curfew enforced by electronic monitoring.

Only defendants facing an immediate sentence of imprisonment are supposed to become subject to court orders relating to treatment, and they are supposed to consent to the order. Nevertheless, as new methods of drug monitoring are introduced, it may be that many defendants agree to quite intrusive monitoring of medical treatment in order to stay out of prison. The distinction between treatment (something tailored to the needs of the individual) and supervision (carried out through the work of court officers such as probation officers) may become quite blurred. The status of information disclosed by defendants during the course of treatment may become relatively unclear.

Hopefully, the potential dangers involved in 'networking' are understood by professionals, who will organise their work accordingly. Nevertheless, work involving the disclosure of sensitive information to different professionals who have the capacity to take sanctions against drug users has a potential to be threatening to those being processed by such systems.

## FREEDOM FROM DISCRIMINATION

Stereotyped images of cocaine use and cocaine users have been common – we are all familiar with the old image of rock stars and other affluent people with gargantuan appetites for cocaine. More recent public images pressed upon us have been those of high levels of US-style crack use among black youth. These generalisations are dangerous, often racist, and frequently entirely counterproductive resulting in, for example, inappropriate policing of communities.

Such images allow for the stigmatisation of cocaine users, which can cause real difficulties. Inevitably, the legal status of cocaine and some other drugs means that consumers will be reluctant to divulge a history of cocaine use to strangers. Professionals providing services to casual drug users will usually have no idea that drug use has occurred. If such use is divulged, it may be difficult for professionals to keep a sense of proportion, and to respond without focusing unnecessarily on the illicit drug use. Blaming the cocaine user, rather than dealing with, say, a routine primary health care problem, brings its own difficulties, and means that it may be difficult for users to gain access to different types of services, or have their difficulties assessed fairly.


## CONCLUSION

The threat posed by cocaine and other drugs has been used to justify a number of measures that infringe individual liberties directly through increased police and judicial powers and, indirectly, through use of increasingly intrusive monitoring of private citizens by professionals by use of drug checks in employment, for example. Whether such measures will actually eradicate cocaine use is arguable. The stakes have certainly been raised by emergency legislation passed to deal with the alleged threat posed by drugs. But as sanctions have been taken against drug users and drug dealers, the world of drug dealing generally has become a nastier, uglier place. Violent crimes now take place, as dealers protect different drug territories.

Individuals continue to use cocaine, which is still available cheaply and in quantity. Indeed, illegal drug use is once again fashionable. In the long term, our collective sacrifice of freedom and privacy may be seen as a futile gesture in support of unenforceable panic measures.

## NOTES

1. See Robertson, G. *Freedom, the Individual and the Law* (Hasmonds-worth: Pelican, 1989), p. 11.
2. See 'Criminalizing Pregnancy – the Downside of a Kinder Gentler Nation', *Social Justice*, Vol. 17, 3, 1990, pp. 111–23.
3. See Stimson, G., 'British Drug Policies in the '80's' in *Drug Misuse – A Reader*, ed. Hetter *et al.* (Chichester: Wiley Medical, 1987), p. 123.
4. Ibid.
5. Culminating in the production of the report *Aids and Drug Misuse, Part 1, Report by the Advisory Council on the Misuse of Drugs* (London: HMSO, 1988), which set out goals of 'harm reduction' in dealing with drug users.
6. From transcript of R. Stutman's speech to the 9th Annual National Drugs Conference of Assistant Chief Police Officers, April 1989.
7. See Loren Siegel, American Civil Liberties Union, 'The Criminalization of Pregnant and Child Rearing Users', unpublished paper presented to International Conference on the Reduction of Drug Related Harm, Liverpool, 1990.
8. Ibid.
9. See Wisotsky, S., *Breaking the Impasse in the War on Drugs* (New York: Greenwood Press, 1987), pp. 116–39.
10. See Feldman, D̄., *Criminal Confiscation Orders – the New Law* (London: Butterworth, 1988), p. 106.
11. See Kay, L., 'Aramah and the Street Value of drugs', *CLR*, 1987, pp. 118–125.
12. See 'Criminalizing Pregnancy – the Downside of a Kinder Gentler Nation', *Social Justice*, Vol. 17, 3, 1990, pp. 111–23.
13. Perry, L., 'Fit to be Parents?', *Druglink*, January, 1987, p. 6.
14. Dubble, Dun, Aldridge and Kearney, 'Registering Concern' in *Community Care*, 12 March 1987, p. 2.

# 7 Treatment of Cocaine Abuse: Exploring the Condition and Selecting the Response

## John Strang, Michael Farrell and Sujata Unnithan

### WHAT IS THE NATURE OF THE PROBLEM?

Any consideration of treatment must necessarily be preceded by a consideration of the condition for which the treatment may possibly be indicated. Consideration of treatment does not require the condition to be seen as a disease or illness – the term remains useful across a wide range of conditions as diverse as a broken leg, bereavement, baldness and sunburn. However, concerns about drug use will differ according to the nature of the drug-using population, the society in which this drug use takes place, and the standpoint of the observer who experiences the concern; and in only some of these cases will the concept of treatment be appropriate.

Central to much of the current confusion and debate is the uncertainty about the criteria which define a suitable case for treatment. From the heterogeneous population of individuals who may have used one or more drugs, towards which of these individuals might treatments (medical, social, public health, etc.) be legitimately directed? In the UK, drug workers and users will often refer to different levels of relationship with drug use as being either as experimental, recreational or compulsive/dependent.

*Experimental drug users* are led to drug use by curiosity about the nature of the drug and the effect is therefore time-limited – lasting until the knowledge has been obtained. It is mainly peer-group activity and is unlikely to be associated with any pharmacological drive to seek the particular drug effect.

*Recreational drug users* are those who, having experimented with drugs, continue to take drugs in order to obtain a known effect (typically perceived as positive at this stage).

*Compulsive/dependent drug users* are those recreational users who develop dependence and/or other problems; for example, the dominant position of pursuit and use of the drug may be accompanied by a tolerance of damage to personal or family well-being and as the use of the drug becomes a more exclusive pursuit and activity it may no longer be associated with the pursuit of positive effects but may be taken for the abolition of negative physical or psychological effects (Yates, 1985).

The problem drug-taker is defined as 'any person who experiences social, psychological, physical or legal problems related to intoxication and/or regular excessive consumption and/or dependence as a consequence of his/her own use of drugs and other chemical substances . . .' (Advisory Council on the Misuse of Drugs, 1982).

Much work has also been done to define more precisely the dependence itself; Edwards and his colleagues have explored this concept widely in the alcohol field (Edwards and Gross, 1976; Stockwell *et al.*, 1979; Stockwell, 1986) and more recently, but less extensively, in the opiate field (Sutherland *et al.*, 1986; Phillips *et al.*, 1987). Often it is mistakenly thought that these two terms and linked areas of understanding merely reflect a medical or sociological term for the same phenomenon. However, when they are studied more closely, it becomes clear that there may be value in considering them as largely independent dimensions (in so far as each of them might legitimately be considered as a single dimension). Consideration of two individual drug users, therefore, might find one scoring highly on problems but low on dependence while, for the second, the loading was reversed.

The many perspectives and levels of understanding of drug use are seen in the diversity of terms. In different centres and with different professions the terms will often be interchanged, as though they merely reflect current fashion and one group's penchant for a particular term. Often, however, this approach fails to provide clarification for the different component parts of the drug-taking behaviour which are the subject of treatment or study. In an effort to identify a limited set of terms and concepts which consensus might form, the World Health Organisation prepared a memorandum on terminology. In this, Edwards *et al.* (1981) put forward proposals for more specific terms for the various phenomena under study. Terms such as 'abuse' and 'misuse' seemed pejorative and hence unsatisfactory in a scientific context. They suggested that the underlying meaning could be more effectively conveyed by using the following four terms:

(i) *Unsanctioned use:* use of a drug that is not approved by a society, or a group within that society. When the term is used, it should be made clear who is responsible for the disapproval. The term implies that we accept disapproval as a fact in its own right without having to determine or justify the basis of that disapproval.

(ii) *Hazardous use:* use of a drug that will probably lead to harmful consequences for the user – either dysfunction or harm. This concepts is similar to the idea of risky behaviour. For instance, smoking 20 cigarettes each day may not be accompanied by any present or actual harm but we know it to be hazardous.

(iii) *Dysfunctional use:* use of a drug that is leading to impaired psychological or social functioning (e.g. loss of job or marital problems).

(iv) *Harmful use:* use of a drug that is known to have caused tissue damage or mental illness in the particular person.

Edwards *et al.* take up the increasing dissatisfaction with the apparent division between physical dependence and psychological psychic dependence. They suggested the use of the term 'neuroadaptation', which covers the changes associated with physical and psychological withdrawal phenomena and also with the development of tolerance. Thus neuroadaptation covers the cellular, metabolic and behaviour adaptations to use and to continued use of the drug. It may also be extended to the concept of reciprocal neuroadaptation to describe the phenomenon previously described as cross-tolerance.

Thus the issue of caseness would not seem to be simple binary phenomenon either on or off, either present or absent. There may be public health or education interventions for one drug user (e.g. public information about the risks of needle-sharing for the occasional hedonistic injector) which may need to be considered across a different population from more orthodox treatment populations (e.g. the regular cocaine user who has become dependent). It is not that one type of case has disappeared as another has been defined: rather what is required is a careful scrutiny of the potential target population while considering the potential benefits (and harms) which may result from proposed and existing interventions.

## WHAT IS THE NATURE OF THE TREATMENT?

Much of the treatments which might be appropriate for the cocaine user are not specific to cocaine but are, in fact, elements drawn from the broad principles of treatment and rehabilitation of drug abusers. Thus harm-minimisation approaches and techniques of motivational interviewing and relapse prevention may appropriately be applied in the management of cocaine users in just the same way as with other drug users; whereas other elements of the provision of treatment such as differential diagnosis and detoxification methods may be specific to consideration of cocaine itself. In reality, there is overlap between these two groups of considerations – for example, consideration of detoxification will include elements of consideration which are common to all drugs, while there will also be additional consideration of strategies which are specific to cocaine. Both general and specific elements are considered in the later sections of this chapter.

Consideration of treatment must also extend beyond narrow concepts of medical care. Consider, for example, the benefits that have been demonstrated from contingency contracting (Bigelow *et al.*, 1980; Anker and Crowley, 1982; and Crowley, 1984), or from manipulating the environment in which the drug user lives or to which the drug user returns after a period of residential care (see Hawkins, 1983). Consider also equivalent work in which re-enforcers in the environment are identified and then manipulated to encourage the continued abstinence of recovering alcoholics – for example in the series of studies from Azrin and colleagues (1982). Perhaps not treatment out of a bottle, but each of these different approaches represents a deliberate intervention designed to bring about a predictable improvement in the outcome of the condition under treatment.

## THE GOALS OF TREATMENT

Stable abstinence is a worthy goal: but a practitioner or programme which is only willing to work with drug users who agree on this immediate goal may miss many an opportunity to bring about improvements in the physical, psychological and social conditions of drug users with whom they come in contact. While going for total abstinence may be seen as best, and while anything else may be seen as distinctly second-best, there may be times when going for second-best may be best-first – especially if the result is that this more modest benefit may be achieved in a larger proportion of drug users.

Since the advent of HIV, this broader perspective has come to the fore and has been termed 'harm minimisation' (Buning, 1990; O'Hare *et al.*, 1992; Strang and Farrell 1992; Stimson, in press). It is worth reminding oneself there is nothing new about this consideration of the goals of prevention and of the range of behaviour changes from which benefit results (see, for example, Edwards, 1980; Institute for the Study of Drug Dependence, 1980; Advisory Council on the Misuse of Drugs, 1984); and the idea is particularly well-suited to adoption by the alternative or underground press (e.g. Aldrich, 1991 in the alternative magazine *High Times*; and Gilman, 1992, *Smack in the Eye* comic).


METHOD OF USE

Across the world as well as across the UK, cocaine has been taken in a variety of ways at different times. During the 1960s, the more famous spread of heroin addiction in the UK (which involved pre-scribed or diverted supplies of pharmaceutical heroin) was often accompanied by use of cocaine (prescribed or diverted supplies of pharmaceutical cocaine) – typically, injected together in what came to be known as a 'speedball'. However, within the first year of intro-duction of the NHS drug treatment centres in 1968, the majority of doctors in the new clinics formed the view that the prescribing of injectable cocaine was either inappropriate or unnecessary on a long-term basis – and hence this source of cocaine had largely disappeared by 1970 (see Connell and Strang, in press). (This appears to be an example of considerable success resulting from a supply-side in-tervention, as it was not until more than a decade later that the black-market in imported cocaine began to grow – in a manner that seems entirely independent of the supply-side intervention in the late 1960s). During the 1980s, small quantities of illicitly-manufactured cocaine from South America began to arrive in the UK (see Chapter 2): most of this cocaine was being taken by snorting, with only a small proportion being taken by injection. The taking of cocaine by smok-ing gradually reached public awareness during the mid-1980s, follow-ing reports of freebasing cocaine and crack smoking in the US. Subsequent anecdotal reports have been given to us by drug users indicating that, at least within well-defined parts of the rock-music business, the practice of freebasing cocaine had made its transatlantic passage as early as 1974.

What significance should be attached to the route of administration of the drug? Amid the bustle of activity surrounding the categorisation of cocaine and other illicit drugs, one would be forgiven for thinking that the effects, abuse-potential, dependence-liability and harmful consequences were solely related to the substance itself. In reality, the extent to which cocaine is active in each of these areas may well be significantly related to the route of administration. From the consumer's point of view, great importance is usually attached to the speed of onset of the effect and the nature of that effect. The blast from intravenous use of cocaine has been likened to sexual orgasm, following which there are the more extended effects of euphoria, alertness and increased energy. More recently, the association has become more explicit, with combined sex and drugs activities, including crack-smoking at the point of orgasm – known in the US as a 'masterblaster'. In contrast, the use of the same cocaine by snorting results in a slow onset of effect during 20 to 30 minutes with no immediate 'blast' but with a similar extended euphoria, alertness and energy. When taken by swallowing or by absorption across the buccal mucosa (as in the traditional use of coca by chewing a wad which is then left between gum and cheek to be absorbed slowly) the rate of absorption is even slower and hence a more extended duration of effect is achieved. So what does one see with the new methods of use – the freebasing of cocaine and the smoking of crack–cocaine? The distinctive feature of both these methods of cocaine use are that the cocaine is removed from the encumbrance of its associated salt (the hydrochloride) and so can pass from blood to brain more rapidly; and also that as a result of the removal of the hydrochloride, the cocaine base can now be smoked and absorbed across the lungs where the large surface area results in extensive rapid absorption directly into the venous blood system of the lungs, which is then delivered to the body and the brain without the partial breakdown in the liver (known as first-pass metabolism). In many ways freebasing and crack-smoking might be regarded as intravenous cocaine without the injection. It may then be possible to consider the sequelae of cocaine use according to the route of administration, and to see areas of concern in which new technologies (e.g. freebasing and crack-smoking) may be located with concerns associated with one or other pre-existing route of administration.

PATTERNS OF USE

Cocaine users range from the individual who consumes the drug on a very occasional basis to the compulsive uncontrolled cocaine-user. Over 30 million Americans have tried cocaine intranasally and it is estimated that 80 per cent have not become regular users and that 95 per cent are not addicted to the drug (Gawin *et al.*, 1989). People may start off using only monthly and gradually escalate to weekend use, to daily use and to higher-dose usage and to intense binge use. Careful history-taking is necessary at the intermediate stage of dependence to assess the level of problematic drug use. In particular, there is a common misconception that someone must take a drug daily before they are defined as dependent on it. While many cocaine users may use on a daily basis, many heavy cocaine binges will last for three days, stop for two days and then resume. Such a pattern of use could inadvertently be described as twice-weekly cocaine use. The average cocaine binge lasts approximately 12 hours with the drug being taken every 10–20 minutes over that period of time. The factors influencing the evolution of dependence are unclear, but the establishment of regular recreational use increases vulnerability under the maxim that drug use predicts continued drug use. A shift in route of use from nasal to inhalation or intravenous use is also likely to increase dependence-liability. Intravenous use may involve injecting up to 20 times a day.

Cocaine abstinence follows a three-phase pattern: crash, withdrawal and return (Gawin *et al.*, 1989):

(a) *Crash: immediate withdrawal phase*: This is the opposite of the high phase, and many cocaine users experience marked depressive symptoms, with anxiety, agitation and sleepiness and very little desire to take cocaine.

(b) *Intermediate withdrawal phase*: Users experience significant depressive symptoms with low energy, low appetite and social withdrawal. Mood fluctuations with anxiety and panic attacks, and sometimes suicidal thoughts, increase in intensity at the end of the first drug-free week and this is a period of high vulnerability to relapse. This phase is associated with increased craving for cocaine which may result in renewed cocaine bingeing.

(c) *Return* to baseline mood state will occur if abstinence from cocaine is maintained. This can be associated with episodic intense cocaine-craving.

**Diagnostic Issues**

A substantial minority of cocaine addicts who have contact with treatment services have co-existing pathologies. They may be found to be depressed, to have panic attacks and palpitations, to have difficulties with concentration, to have cardiac irregularities. Some of these will be phenomena which are consequent upon the drug use – either drug side-effects, signs of withdrawal, or consequences of the route of administration (e.g. of injecting). Other phenomena may have a causal significance – i.e. their pre-existence and the effect they exert actually leads to some critical step or change in drug use (perhaps initial use, or subsequent regular use, or the development of dependence).

The nature of the relationship between drug use and psychiatric disorders may be considered as either causal, co-incidental or consequent upon the drug use.

Psychological and psychiatric disorders may be causally implicated in the development of subsequent problem drug use or dependence. Personal developmental and social disorders in childhood are associated with an increased probability of drug dependence in adult life (see Rounsaville *et al.*, 1983, for example), although the strength of such relationships is not sufficient to be predictive. Pre-existing anxiety states or depressive disorders may lead to use of prescribed or illicit drugs as an attempt at self-medication (Khantzian, 1985) or, alternatively, may lead to a reliance on regular use of the drug as a maladaptive coping mechanism. Recent reports from the US have suggested that a small proportion of cocaine addicts may have been previously suffering from Attention Deficit Disorder (ADD), but the true interpretation of the causal relationship has yet to be established. In such cases, consideration should be given to treatment of the primary pathology (e.g. the anxiety state or depressive illness) as well as treatment of the secondary dependence.

Psychiatric disorders may occur independently of the drug use. It is important not to be blinded by the drug dependence. All physical and psychiatric disorders may occur independently in subjects who are drug-dependent, and the drug-dependence may sometimes confuse the clinical picture or mislead the physician in the diagnostic process: clinical vigilance must be preserved, as other pathology may be present in addition to the drug dependence.

Psychiatric disorders may occur which are a direct result of the drug use – they are consequent upon the drug use. These may be conveniently regarded as either (i) drug-induced disorders, or (ii) drug-precipitated disorders.

(i) Drug-induced disorders are those in which the drug use has been directly causally responsible for the development of the illness. The classic example is the drug-induced psychoses associated with stimulant drugs such as the amphetamines (Connell, 1958: Bell, 1965: Ellinwood, 1967) and cocaine (Gordon, 1908; Post, 1975; Cohen, 1984) and, in particular, crack–cocaine (Manschreck *et al.* 1987), in which there is a time-limited short-term psychosis while the drug remains in the system but is not associated with an increased incidence of subsequent psychotic episodes (other than those associated with further drug use). Drug-related psychiatric disorders can also occur as features of the withdrawal syndrome – notably the profound immediate depressive reaction during the first few days after cocaine or amphetamine was last taken and the more protracted (although usually less intense) depression that follows withdrawal of these drugs.

(ii) Drug-precipitated psychiatric disorders are those in which the drug has acted as a trigger to an otherwise independent psychiatric illness. Thus adverse reactions to drug use may act as the life-event which triggers an anxiety state, major depressive or psychotic disorder: the significant point here is that the management and likely time course of the disorder is now dictated by the independent psychiatric condition itself and not by the drug use.

(Additionally, drug use may cause a recurrence of ongoing psychiatric disorders.)

## HARM MINIMISATION

Harm minimisation is effective secondary and tertiary prevention. Clearly, a person will incur no harm from cocaine if they avoid it completely. However, if they do use cocaine they should be fully informed of the risks involved and attempt to ensure that they incur the minimum harm from such behaviour. In particular, people need to understand the risks involved in multiple-drug use and the increased likelihood of drug overdose when a variety of drugs are mixed. Also, recent reports suggest that the combination of alcohol and cocaine results in the liver producing a metabolite named cocaethylene which intensifies cocaine's euphoric effect but may also increase the risk of sudden death.

In the era of HIV it might be thought that a substance that has a high preference for consumption by smoking would reduce risk of HIV transmission from injecting. In the UK there has been an increase in the use of smokable cocaine in preference to intranasal use (Strang *et al.*, 1990). However, in the US such use appears to be related to unsafe sexual behaviour and to increased rates of syphilis and HIV infection. In Amsterdam, a study of injecting drug-users reported lower levels of HIV infection among those with a preference for smoking cocaine and heroin, suggesting that substantial cultural factors may mediate the level of risk behaviour involved in such drug use. Cocaine-injecting, because of its high daily frequency, is associated with an increased rate of HIV seropositivity and is recognised as an independent risk factor for HIV infection.

If cocaine users are injecting frequently, it is useful to ensure that they have information on sources of needless and syringes and that they use 'sharps boxes' to dispose of used equipment. Inadvertent sharing may occur in a situation where the injector is injecting every twenty minutes and reusing syringes. Advice on injection site care should be given.


## HOW THE INTERVIEW CAN ITSELF BE THERAPEUTIC

The therapist may regard the interview (especially the first interview) as an opportunity to gather information about the present history of drug use and associated background, and an opportunity to assess physical, psychological and social aspects and sequelae of the drug use. However, to the patient/client, the consultation is often much more than this: it may be but a period of time in a drug worker's timetable, but to the drug user it may be the first occasion which they have conducted an audit of their drug use and its consequences. The manner in which the therapist steers the interview may be heavily influential on the actions which the drug taker may consider, on the courses which he/she may subsequently follow (including the extent to which they may engage in treatment at that time or on a subsequent occasion). The reality of life as a drugworker is that one should live one's day as if it were one's last: in a consultation with a new client there is no certainty that there will be a second opportunity

to influence that particular individual. UK studies from drug dependence units show that about a third of subjects may drop out of
treatment even before beginning that treatment, with similar substantial losses at later stages in the treatment process (Love and Gossop,
1986; Dawe *et al.*, 1991). Similar figures are evident in analyses of the
work of needle-exchange schemes (Stimson *et al.*, 1988; 1990), with a
third of injectors only attending on one occasion and less than a fifth
attending on more than five occasions. In the treatment of smokers
and problem drinkers, there is impressive evidence of adaptation to
these realities of clinical practice, with the development of brief
intervention strategies such as may be applied by the general practitioner or other therapist who may be uncertain about future contact
or has only limited time during the present contact (Heather, 1987;
1989). Indeed, Edwards and Orford (1977) found such single interventions to be as efficacious as engagement in hospital out-patient
care, in their comparative study of the management of problem
drinkers referred to an alcohol treatment unit. As yet, formal brief
intervention strategies have not been developed for work with
cocaine users or other illicit drug users, but it seems likely that a
similarly realistic approach to the potentially therapeutic benefit of
single interventions should be adopted in working with cocaine users.

The interventions of the therapist may strongly influence the audit
being undertaken by the client. Miller has described an approach of
'motivational interviewing' – initially in the context of working with
problem drinkers, but subsequently adapted to other groups of drug
users. In this approach, one of the covert goals of the therapist is to
generate a critical mass of dissonance in the client so as to increase
their willingness to consider alternatives to continued drug or alcohol
use (Miller, 1983). Although Miller sees this as a complete therapeutic approach in itself, it could alternatively be argued that this
approach represents a useful tool in the repertoire of the versatile
therapist and can be incorporated into various other treatment styles.

## MOTIVATIONAL INTERVIEWING

In this approach motivation is conceptualised as an interpersonal
process in which the therapist has considerable opportunity to influence subsequent attributions and behaviour by the client. Denial is
not simply seen as inherent in the client, but is seen as a product of
the way in which therapist and client interact. The covert aim of

therapy is to generate increasing levels of cognitive dissonance until a critical mass of motivation is achieved – at which point the drug taker becomes willing to consider change alternatives. Miller emphasises that the therapist should initially adopt an empathic stance (using the classical techniques described by Carl Rogers). However, the 'business' of the approach occurs when this process is subtly modified so that the reflective function of the therapist is moulded so as to reinforce statements of concern and elicit self-motivational statements from the client – an approach that has more recently been described as positively Machiavellian (Gossop and Strang, 1990)! Ownership of the items elicited must rest with the client, who is assisted in constructing an inventory of problems related to their drug use, and possible change alternatives – often by completion of a matrix of advantages/disadvantages and drug use/abstinence, or a cost benefit analysis (Janis and Mann, 1977). If the therapist is effective, then the client will be unaware of the subtle distortion in the original reflective listening of the therapist. The therapist is advised to use the client's own language, whenever possible, so as to increase the extent of self-attribution and personal ownership of the concerns which emerge. In this way, history-taking in interview is seen not only as a means of obtaining information and background, but also as a means of influencing the client in the identification of problems and in the consideration of change alternatives. The work has subsequently been adapted for work with heroin addicts (Van Bilsen and Van Emst, 1986; Van Bilsen, 1988) and it seems reasonable to presume that the approach could similarly be adapted to work with cocaine users.

## THE PROVISION OF SPECIFIC TREATMENTS

### Detoxification

Detoxification from opiates with marked physical withdrawal symptoms requires gradually reducing dosage of opiates. However, the lack of physical sequelae in cocaine withdrawal renders it a simpler drug to detoxify from. A clear understanding of the nature of the psychological sequelae of cocaine withdrawal is required if appropriate support is to be given to someone who is withdrawing from cocaine.

The first four to six weeks of detoxification aims to rapidly establish a cocaine-free state and to provide support when acute urges to consume the drug occur. Acute medical or psychiatric complications such as convulsions or acute anxiety or depression should be monitored for. It is also during this early phase that chemical treatments to reduce cocaine withdrawal symptoms can be commenced.

Previous studies have shown that long-term cocaine use depletes the key monoamines at the synaptic cleft. In addition, it appears that the brain receptors become more sensitive (Branch and Dearing, 1982). Both of these changes in brain function are known to be associated with depression and loss of energy. These two features and the craving associated are often seen in the withdrawal phase. It seems likely therefore that anti-depressants would counteract this problem.

Studies suggest that the anti-depressant desipramine is particularly helpful in reducing the depression and craving of cocaine withdrawal (O'Brien *et al.*, 1988). The advantages of using this drug include: relatively few toxic side-effects and therefore increased likelihood of treatment compliance. The disadvantages include the fact that the onset of action may be 10–20 days after starting treatment, and blood tests are required to check that the blood-level of drug is therapeutic. Treatment using desipramine is usually for three months with the drug being taken at night and the dose gradually being reduced. Desipramine may also reduce craving for cocaine, a common reason for early lapse to use. Bromocryptine is a dopamine agonist and it has been speculated that, for this reason, it might act as an anti-craving agent (Dakis *et al.*, 1986).

To summarise, no one specific method of pharmacological treatment exists for detoxification from cocaine. Certain drugs, however, namely desipramine and bromocryptine, appear helpful in reducing powerful withdrawal symptoms. This, in turn, may help the cocaine user to remain drug-free.

**Relapse Prevention**

Relapse prevention is a cognitive behavioural treatment strategy directed at enhancing an individual's capacity to sustain a durable change in behaviour. However, within 90 days of treatment of a drug problem, two-thirds of the treated individuals will have reused drugs (Hunt *et al.*, 1971).

This breakdown in the individual's attempt to remain drug-free is termed a 'lapse'. It may be viewed in two ways; as catastrophic and therefore leading to more drug use, or as a learning experience, concentrating on the potential pitfalls of daily life and the need to acquire new coping skills. This latter process is the basis for much of the work of Relapse Prevention (Marlatt and George, 1984).

Actual use of the drug is only the final point in a longer process. Events leading to a lapse to cocaine are explained in terms of a high-risk situation (Cummings *et al.*, 1980) which may include: interpersonal conflict, negative mood-states, being in a situation where the drug is readily available, viewing the state of being drug-free at the end of detoxification as signifying the end of treatment (Washton, 1988). Learning new coping skills to cope with high-risk situations may reduce the likelihood of relapse. Dependent cocaine users test their own control by attempting occasional use of cocaine, which usually leads to a relapse to dependent use. Anticipation of risks and rehearsal of coping strategies are therefore central to Relapse Prevention.

If lapse occurs, the psychological reaction to it is crucial. Cocaine users who view themselves as having lost control are more likely to recommence regular use, compared to the person who sees such an episode of use as a lapse requiring further concerted effort to learn and enhance Relapse-Prevention coping skills.

Specific coping techniques include: describing past relapse situations, imagining high-risk situations, and role-play with other users to avoid use (Annis and Davis, 1988). Importance is also placed on education about drug dependence and the risk of lapse and negative consequences of cocaine use, i.e. physical complications. Acknowledgement is given to the fact that an urge to use may suddenly occur, but strategies of distraction and relaxation are taught, to counteract this.

The process of lapse begins with the cocaine user being presented with a high-risk situation. Relapse Prevention aims at the development of coping strategies to prevent lapse. If, however, a lapse does occur, it should not be regarded as failure of treatment. Instead, it should be used to learn new mechanisms to prevent further lapse leading to full blown dependent use.

## Individual Psychotherapy

Most structured group or individual work with dependent drug users initially needs to concentrate on consolidating a drug-free state. Individual cognitive behavioural approaches such as Relapse Prevention are most clearly focused to this end. However, separate individual therapy may be required such as cognitive therapy for depression or behaviour therapy for persistent anxiety states; concomitantly, non-specific supportive psychotherapy, social skills training or assertiveness training may be appropriate.

The main goals for any form of individual psychotherapy are to encourage more self-awareness, learn new adaptive skills and increase self-esteem (Rounsaville *et al.*, 1985). Dynamic or insight-orientated psychotherapy may be of considerable benefit to individuals to process traumatic past events such as sexual abuse, physical abuse and neglect and early parental loss or other developmental disruptions. However, on balance, such an approach is best reserved until substantial progress has been made at consolidating a drug-free state and acquiring substantial social stability.

**Family Work**

The recruitment of families to treatment is the first hurdle. Marital issues in isolation, however, are delayed until problems within the larger family are dealt with. Spouses, at this stage, more commonly enter support groups rather than analytical groups.

The three main types of family therapy involve emphasis on different psychological mechanisms, although all aim eventually for a change in behaviour of the family (Stanton, 1979). Psychodynamic approaches involve understanding the origins of the problem, relating this to family development. Analysis of the items revealed is thought to help introduce change. Behavioural methods concentrate on emphasising assertiveness and alternative behavioural reactions to the drug-using family member. A 'systems' approach examines a family structure which may encourage continued drug-use. Those families who avoid conflict, for example, will be encouraged to discuss and deal with difficult issues relating to the cocaine addiction and the individual.

At the initial interview the treatment aims are planned. Included in the discussion will be realistic goals, assessment of family structure, strengths of the family and their knowledge of the problem. The therapist who will supervise the sessions will need to enquire if family members can describe patterns of use, financing methods and behaviour change.

Following the initial meeting, a contract of treatment goals is drawn up, including basic rules on who will attend. Emphasis is placed on regular drug-free attendance (monitored by urine samples to check for presence of drugs). One-to-one sessions, involving the therapist and one member of the family, are discouraged. Although the therapist will have established authority over the sessions, interaction is aimed at helping rather than directing the family to change. This is done by helping to interpret feelings such as self-blame as concern, and helping to change the balance of power in the family system.

Family groups provide the chance to allow ventilation of feelings, reduce the feeling of isolation and understand how a family may inadvertently facilitate drug use (Spitz and Rosencan, 1987). Relapse may occur during family therapy, particularly where a change in the family system has occurred. The crisis can, however, be used as a learning experience for the whole family, examining, perhaps, any interaction which may have been precipitated.

At the end of the sessions, a review of the experience is performed and emphasis is placed on the fact that support can be maintained and that there will be follow-up with support groups. Family support is also available through the family support organisations such as Families Anonymous and ADFAM.

**Twelve-step Programmes**

Twelve-step programmes are outgrowths from the original Alcoholic Anonymous groups where the steps refer to the stages that an individual needs to go through to achieve sobriety. People who are affiliated to AA generally describe themselves as recovering, on the basis that the underlying philosophy views addiction as an illness for which there is no cure. Narcotics Anonymous was started in San Francisco in 1953 and has slowly grown to be a large international movement with substantial growth in Europe during the 1980s.

The main activity of NA is the organisation of meetings, which are attended by people who have experienced drug-related problems, and who come together to provide mutual self-help to maintain a drug-free state. Meetings may be closed, for drug-users only, or open, where families or other interested professionals may attend. Meetings last 90 minutes, with the first 40 minutes taken up with one person describing their life-story and others subsequently adding in with their own experience. Most large cities now have a wide network of meetings that take place virtually every lunch-time and every evening, so that an immense amount of support is available through this extensive self-help network. More recently, separate groups for cocaine-users, titled Cocaine Anonymous, have been established in the US, but this has not occurred in the UK and in general seems to encourage a fragmentation of response to the broader issue of addiction and dependence. However, there may be a place for such a division, where young, non-injecting drug users wish to make contact with self-help groups and where one would feel a reluctance to encourage them to become involved with a wider network of previous injecting drug users with the risk that education on aspects of injecting drug use may be counterproductive and move people down the pathway of injecting drug use. However, such a view may be paternalistic and overprotective. Some cocaine users report that the differences between cocaine and opiate-use are such that Anonymous groups that specifically address the problems of stimulant dependence are very helpful. Cocaine users may also have experience of major alcohol-related problems and find some help and support in the fellowship of Alcoholics Anonymous. Many drug users will not wish to use such self-help groups; however, it is generally advisable to suggest to users new to treatment that they attend at least two or three separate meetings to find out if they can obtain any benefit from such meetings. Drug users who have experienced parental drug or alcohol problems may find some help in also attending Adult Children of Alcoholics groups or similar such support groups.

Much of the self-help movement is based in the community but many drug users may be initially introduced to it in an inpatient or therapeutic community setting. (For further consideration, see Wells, 1992.)

**Rehabilitation Programmes**

In the UK, the majority of rehabilitation programmes are residentially-based. However, there is now considerable interest in the development of intensive non-residential day programmes. The broad model of treatment in the therapeutic community uses self-help in a drug-free environment, where the residents play a substantial role in the day-to-day running. It emphasises personal responsibility and provides a structure where members only advance through achievements (Kerr, 1986). In particular, the confrontational style aims to provide residents with firm feedback on their behaviour and to establish clear set behaviour limits. The original therapeutic community was established after the Second World War by Maxwell

Jones. Then in the United States a group of ex-drug users established communities based on harsh confrontational approaches which, to the disbelief of many external observers, had a major beneficial impact on many of the residents. Rosenthal then established the Phoenix House therapeutic community in New York and a similar community was established in South London in the sixties. There is now a network of these treatment facilities, broadly termed Concept houses. These are long-term residential communities with expected stays of 12 to 18 months. These settings are organised in a structured hierarchical fashion, in which people work from the bottom to the top of a whole sequence of hierarchies, which are involved in the day-to-day running of the community (see Rosenthal, 1990).

The second commonest treatment programme is the Minnesota Model short-term residential community which is based on the AA/NA Twelve-step model with expected length of stay of eight weeks with follow-on to halfway support houses. Christian-style religious communities are the third style. These communities do not insist that residents follow Christian religious practice but believe that religion is a potential key dimension of recovery. There are no clear criteria or outcome studies to suggest who can benefit best from the different styles of treatment. Length of stay in treatment is the best predictor of positive treatment outcome (De Leon 1984).

There is a need for improved links between the residential treatment sector and the mental health services. Many cases of clinical depression may go unrecognised and untreated and stimulants may precipitate or aggravate major psychiatric disorder. There is a need for a more structured approach to such problems and these problems may be concentrated among cocaine users. Some units have also developed mother-and-baby units or family units in an attempt to increase drug-using families' possibilities of staying together.

## POST-DETOX PHARMACOLOGICAL STRATEGIES

Prescribing drugs as a way of reducing drug use often attracts adverse criticism from outside commentators – and quite rightly so, unless the likely benefits outweigh the inherent paradox. So when might the prescribing of drugs be considered within drug treatment programmes? The provision of drugs for detoxification has already been considered earlier in this chapter; as has the possibility of prescribing drugs in the context of a harm-minimisation approach.

An alternative approach might be the use of a substitute opiate, comparable to the use of oral methadone as a maintenance drug for opiate addicts. However, no candidate drug has yet been identified. Replacement supplies of intravenous cocaine were prescribed by private doctors during the 1960s in the UK and during the first year of the new NHS drug clinics, but the lack of any apparent benefits soon resulted in cessation of this practice. Briefly, during 1968–69, replacement supplies of injectable methylamphetamine (Methedrin) were prescribed initially by private doctors and then by at least one NHS clinic in the UK (Hawks *et al.*, 1969; Mitcheson *et al.*, 1976), but the practitioners concluded that their experience was 'largely a record of therapeutic failing' (De Alarcon, 1972). Despite the preliminary reports of use of methylphenidate (Ritalin) (Khantzian, 1985; Khantzian *et al.*, 1984), it must be borne in mind that this effect may not be constant or predictable (see Gawin *et al.*, 1985), may only be applicable to patients with pre-existing Attention Deficit Disorder (ADD) (Khantzian *et al.*, 1984) and that the drug has an established place in the UK black-market where the tablets have been frequently crushed and injected during the last decade.

Tricyclic anti-depressant drugs (in particular desipramine) are frequently used in the post-detoxification after-care of former cocaine addicts. This is partly because the cocaine use may represent an attempt at self-medication of an underlying depression, but may also be related to the actual mode of action of cocaine and to the neuroadaptation which occurs following regular use of the drug. In the central nervous system (in particular, along biochemical pathways known as the dopamine system) repeated regular use of cocaine leads to changes in synaptic activity – the activity which occurs when one nerve cell fires across a gap to trigger off the electrical impulse in the next nerve, just as the environment may influence the firing and adequacy of the spark in a spark plug. Repeated administration of cocaine leads to a heightened sensitivity in several of these key pathways ('up regulation') which may account for some of the protracted withdrawal syndrome, and which may be reversed by tricyclic anti-depressants such as desipramine (Gawin and Kleber, 1984; Gawin *et al.*, 1989).

If a drug could be found which actually reduced the experience of craving after withdrawal off drugs (or indeed during times of continued drug use) then this drug might possibly be a valuable adjunct to existing treatment approaches. As yet no drug has been identified with the effect of reducing craving in any reliable and acceptable way, other than other obvious substitute drugs which bring with them their own problems of dependence and abuse. However, some drugs are currently the subject of study as possible anti-craving drugs, including bromocryptine (Dakis *et al.*, 1987; Tennant and Sagherian, 1987) and lithium carbonate (Cronson and Flenenbaum, 1978; Gawin and Kleber, 1984).

The final possible point at which a pharmacological strategy may be effective could be with the development of a specific cocaine antagonist similar to the development of naltrexone with the opiates or the recently-developed specific antagonist for the benzodiazepines. It is likely that if and when such a product is developed, it will not be the single magic bullet which the public, politicians and pharmaceutical manufacturers seek, although it may be a valuable additional tool within the armamentarium of the therapist.

## BEHAVIOUR THERAPY: CUE EXPOSURE AND RESPONSE PREVENTION

Behavioural treatments have revolutionised the treatment of many psychological and psychiatric disorders – notably phobias and obsessive compulsive disorders. To what extent might it be applicable to drug use? (For recent commentary on the extent of generalisability of these approaches see Marks, 1990; and subsequent responses from Bradley, 1990; Jaffe, 1990). The approaches were first applied in the alcohol field, with programmes designed to identify the individual signals or cues for drinking, moving on to the systematic exposure of the client to these cues while assisting in avoiding the response (drinking) (see Hodgson, 1982). These cues may be internal feelings (e.g. anxiety or depression) or external events (meeting a group of friends, the sight or smell of the favourite drink, etc.). The aim is to break down the stimulus–response (S–R) relationship which has developed to these cues without the associated response of drinking – initially in a laboratory setting and subsequently *in vivo*. A similar approach has been used with heroin addicts (O'Brien *et al.*, 1974; Childress *et al.*, 1986; Powell *et al.*, 1990), with whom there is certainly extensive evidence of powerful conditioned responses, whose power can certainly be muted in the laboratory setting by repeated exposure. However, the extent to which this benefit will then generalise to a real-life setting remains uncertain. The approach has more recently been applied to cocaine addicts (Childress *et al.*, 1988), with encouraging preliminary results (especially when the basic technique is accompanied by education in 'coping with craving' techniques).

## COMPLICATIONS

In the late 1970s it was assumed that cocaine presented minimal physical or psychological complications. However, the steep rise in consumption among the US population and the subsequent demand on medical and psychiatric emergency services has proved this wrong.

Cocaine has now been shown to cause a wide range of physical problems (Cregler and Marks 1986), ranging from acute cocaine toxicity, with convulsions and possibly death, to less dose-related phenomena such as cardiovascular complications such as myocardial infractions, cardiac rhythm disorders, acute hypertension and brain haemorrhages.

Complications of the mode of administration are aptly titled technique-specific complications and range from nasal septal ulceration from intranasal use, burns from freebasing using ether, and infective complications such as HIV and AIDS from injecting drug use.

Psychological complications range from a dose-related stimulant psychosis, which generally resolves rapidly when cocaine or amphetamine consumption is discontinued, to depressive disorders due to long-term stimulant use and stimulant withdrawal. The acute phase of withdrawal may be associated with substantially increased risk of suicide in depressed (and also not previously depressed) individuals, and precautions to prevent suicide may need to be instituted.

## LOOKING TO THE FUTURE

So what does the future hold in store? Global production of cocaine has increased by at least one order of magnitude during the 1980s, and there are certainly indications of significant increases in the per capita consumption of cocaine in several Western European countries during the late 1980s and early 1990s. However, the relationship between this increased consumption and consequent health problems and dependence remains unclear. Future studies may need to pay greater attention to the different forms of cocaine, the different routes by which it may be taken, the different relationships which may exist with the drug, and the different profiles of problems with which cocaine users may present. A treatment approach which is insensitive to these individual characteristics may satisfy public calls for miracle solutions which are universally applicable, but will be in grave danger of failing to harness the true power of existing treatment approaches, as well as those currently in development.

REFERENCES

Advisory Council on the Misuse of Drugs (1982) (Report on) *Treatment and Rehabilitation* (London: HMSO).
—— (1984) (Report on) *Prevention* (London: HMSO).
Aldrich, M. R. (1991) 'Cocaine Confidential: Nose Care', *High Times*, Vol. 69, May 1981, (Farmingdale, New York: Trans-high Corporation), pp. 42–3.
Anglin, M. D. and McGlothlin, W. H. (1988) 'Outcome of Narcotic Addict Treatment, California', in Timms, F. M. and Ludford, J. P. (eds), *Drug Abuse Treatment Evaluation: Strategies, Progress and Prospects.* NIDA Research Monograph 51 (Rockville, Maryland: National Institute on Drug Abuse).
Anker, A. L. and Crowley, E. J. (1982) 'Use of Contingency Contracting in Specialty Clinics for Cocaine Abuse', in Harris, L. S. (ed.) *Problems of Drug Dependence 1981*, NIDA Research Monograph number 41 (Rockville, Maryland: National Institute on Drug Abuse), pp. 452–9.
Annis, H. M. and Davis, C. S. (1988) 'Assessment of expectancies', in *Assessment of Addictive Behaviours* (New York: Guildford Press), pp. 84–111.
Azrin, N. H., Sisson, R. W., Meyers, R. and Godley, M. (1982) 'Alcoholism treatment by disulfiram and community reinforcement therapy', *Journal of Behaviour Therapy and Experimental Psychiatry*, 13: pp. 105–12.
Bell, D. S. (1965) 'Comparison of Amphetamine Psychosis and Schizophrenia', *British Journal of Psychiatry*, 111: pp. 701–7.
Bigelow, G. E., Stitzer, M. L., Lawrence, C., Krasnegor, N., d'Lugoff, B. and Hawthorne, J. W. (1980) 'Narcotic addiction treatment: behavioural methods concurrent with methadone maintenance', *International Journal of the Addictions*, 15: pp. 427–37.
Bradley, B. (1990) 'Behavioural addictions: common features and treatment implications', *British Journal of Addiction*, 85: pp. 1417–20.
Branch, M. N. and Dearing, M. E. (1982) 'Effects of acute and daily cocaine administration on performance in a delayed matching to sample procedure', *Pharmacology and Biochemistry of Behaviour*, 16(5): pp. 713–18.
Buning, E. (1990) 'The role of harm-reduction programmes in curbing the spread of HIV by drug injectors', in Strang, J. and Stimson, G. (eds) *AIDS and Drug Misuse: the challenge for policy and practice in the 1990s* (London: Routledge), pp. 153–61.

Childress, A. R., McLellan, A. T., and O'Brien, C. P. (1986) 'Abstinent opiate abusers exhibited conditioned craving, conditioned withdrawal and reductions in both through extinction', *British Journal of Addiction*, 81: pp. 655–60.

Childress, A. R., Ehrman, R., McLellan, A. T. and O'Brien, C. P. (1988) 'Conditioned craving and arousal in cocaine addiction', *Problems of Drug Dependence*, NIDA Research Monograph Series (Rockville, Maryland: National Institute on Drug Abuse) pp. 74–80.

Cohen, S. (1984) 'Cocaine: Acute Medical and Psychiatric Complications', *Psychiatric Annals*, 14: pp. 747–9.

Connell, P. H. (1958) *Amphetamine Psychosis*, Maudsley Monograph number 5 (London: Oxford University Press).

Connell, P. H. and Strang, J. 'The drug crisis and the formation of the clinics', in Strang, J. and Gossop, M. (eds), *Responding to Drug Misuse: the 'British System'* (Oxford: Oxford University Press (in press)).

Cregler, L. and Mark, H. (1986) 'Medical complications of cocaine abuse' *New England Journal of Medicine*, 315: pp. 1495–1500.

Cronson, A. J. and Flenenbaum, A. (1978) 'Antagonism of Cocaine Highs by Lithium', *American Journal of Psychiatry*, 135(7): pp. 856–7.

Crowley, T. (1984) *Contingency Contracting Treatment of Drug Abusing Physicians: Nurses' and Dentists' Behavioural Intervention Techniques in Drug Abuse Treatment*, NIDA Research Monograph 46 (Rockville, Maryland: National Institute on Drug Abuse) pp. 58–83.

Cummings, C., Gordon, J. R. and Marlatt, G. A. (1980) 'Relapse: strategies of prevention and prediction', in Miller, W. R. (ed.) *The Addictive Behaviours: Treatment of alcoholism, drug abuse, smoking and obesity* (Oxford: Pergamon Press), pp. 291–315.

De Alarcon, R. (1972) 'An Epidemiological Evaluation of the Public Health Measure Aimed at Reducing the Availability of Methylamphetamine, *Psychological Medicine*, 2: pp. 293–300.

De Leon, G. (1984) 'Programme-based evaluation research in therapeutic communities', in Timms, F. M. and Ludford, J. P. (eds), *Drug Abuse Treatment Evaluation: Strategies, progress and prospects*, NIDA Research Monograph 51 (Rockville, Maryland: National Institute on Drug Abuse) pp. 69–87.

Dackis, C. A., Gold, M. S., Sweeney, D. R., Byron, J. P. and Climko, R. (1986) 'Single dose bromocryptine reverses cocaine craving', *Psychiatry Research*, 20: pp. 261–4.

Dackis, C., Gold, M. S. and Sweeney, D. *et al.* (1987) 'Single dose bromocryptine reverses cocaine craving', *Psychiatry Research*, 20: pp. 261–4.

Dawe, S., Griffiths, P., Gossop, M. and Strang, J. (1991) 'Should opiate addicts be involved in controlling their own detoxification? A comparison of fixed versus negotiable schedules', *British Journal of Addiction*, 86: pp. 977–1042.

Edwards, G. and Gross, M. (1976) 'Alcohol dependence: provisional description of a clinical syndrome', *British Medical Journal*, 1: pp. 1058–1061.

Edwards, G. and Orford, J. (1977) *Alcoholism: A comparison of treatment and advice*, Maudsley Monograph No. 26 (London: Oxford University Press).

Edwards, G. (1980) 'Prevention and the Balance of Strategies', in Edwards, G. and Arif, A. (eds), *Drug Problems in the Sociocultural Context: A basis for policies and programme planning* (Geneva: World Health Organisation).

Edwards, G., Arif, A. and Hodgson, R. (1981) 'Nomenclature and classification of drug and alcohol related problems: a shortened version of a WHO Memorandum', *British Journal of Addiction*, 77: pp. 287–306.

Ellinwood, E. H. (1967) Amphetamine Psychosis: Description of the individuals and process, *Journal of Nervous and Mental Diseases*, 144: pp. 273–83.

Gawin, F. H. and Kleber, H. D. (1984) 'Cocaine Abuse Treatment: Open Pilot Trial with desipramine and lithium carbonate', *Archives of General Psychiatry*, 41(9): pp. 903–9.

Gawin, F. H., Riordan, C. E. and Kleber, H. (1985) 'Methylphenedate Treatment of Cocaine Abusers without Attention Deficit Disorder: A negative report', *American Journal of Drug and Alcohol Abuse*, 2: pp. 193–7.

Gawin, F. H., Kleber, H. D., Byck, R. *et al.* (1989) 'Desipramine Facilitation of Initial Cocaine Abstinence', *Archives of General Psychiatry*, 46: pp. 117–21.

Gilman, M. (1992) 'Smack in the Eye', in O'Hare, P. *et al.* (eds), *The Reduction of Drug Related Harm* (London: Routledge).

Gordon, A. (1908) 'Insanities Caused by the Acute and Chronic Intoxication with Opium and Cocaine', *Journal of the American Medical Association*, 51: pp. 97–101.

Gossop, M. and Strang, J. (1990) 'Psychological Treatments', in Ghodse, H. and Maxwell, D. (eds), *Substance Abuse and Dependence: An introduction for the caring professions* (London: Macmillan).

Hawkins, J. D. (1983) 'Community Characteristics Associated with Treatment Outcome', in Cooper, J. R., Altman, F., Brown, B. S., Czechowicz, D. (eds), *Research on the Treatment of Narcotic Addiction: State of the Art* (Rockville, Maryland: National Institute on Drug Abuse).

Hawks, D. V., Mitcheson, N., Ogbourne, A. and Edwards, G. (1969) 'Abuse of Methylamphetamine', *British Medical Journal*, 2: pp. 715–21.

Hearn, W. L., Flynn, D. D., Hime, G. W. *et al.* (1991) 'Cocaethylene: a unique cocaine metabolite displays high affinity for the dopamine transporter', *Journal of Neurochemistry*, 56: pp. 698–701.

Heather, N. (1987) 'DRAMS for problem drinkers: the potential of a brief intervention by general practitioners and some evidence of its effectiveness', in Stockwell, T. and Clement, S. (eds), *Helping the Problem Drinker: New initiatives in community care* (London: Croom Helm).

—— (1989) 'Psychology and brief interventions', *British Journal of Addiction*, 84: pp. 357–70.

Hodgson, R. (1982) 'Behavioural psychotherapy for compulsions and addictions', in Eiser, J. R. (ed.), *Social Psychology and Behavioural Medicine*, pp. 375–91 (Chichester: Wiley).

Hunt, W. A., Barnett, W. and Branch, L. G. (1971) 'Relapse rates in addiction programme', *Journal of Clinical Psychology*, 27: pp. 455–6.

Institute for the Study of Drug Dependence (1976) 'Not to be sniffed at?', *Druglink*, 6: pp. 1–2 (London: Institute for the Study of Drug Dependence).

—— (1980) 'Teaching about a Volatile Situation: suggested health education strategies for minimising casualties associated with solvent sniffing? (London: ISDD).

Jaffe, J. (1990) 'Trivialising dependence', *British Journal of Addiction*, 85: pp. 1425–8.

Janis, I. and Mann, L. (1977) *Decision-making: a psychological analysis of conflict, choice and commitment* (London: Collier-Macmillan).

Kerr, D. H. (1986) 'The therapeutic community: a codified concept for training and upgrading staff members in a residential setting', in de Leon, G. and Ziegenfuss, J. T. (eds), *Therapeutic Communities for Addictions* (Springfield, Illinois: Charles C. Thomas) pp. 55–64.

Khantzian, E. J., Gawin, F., Kleber, H. D., and Riordan, C. E. (1984) 'Methylphenidate (Ritalin) Treatment of Cocaine Dependence: A Preliminary Report', *Journal of Substance Abuse Treatment*, 1(2): pp. 107–12.

Khantzian, E. J. (1985) 'The Self-Medication Hypothesis of Addictive Disorders: Focus on Heroin and Cocaine Dependence', *American Journal of Psychiatry*, 142(11): pp. 1259–64.

Love, J. and Gossop, M. (1986) 'The processes of referral and disposal within a London Drug Dependence Clinic', *British Journal of Addiction*, 80: pp. 435–40.

Manschreck, T. C., Allen, D. F. and Neville, M. (1987) 'Free-base Psychosis: Cases from a Bahamian Epidemic of Cocaine', *Comprehensive Psychiatry*, 28(6): pp. 555–64.

Marks, I. (1987) *Fears, Phobias and Rituals: Panic, anxiety and their disorders* (New York: Oxford University Press).

—— (1990) 'Behavioural (non-chemical) addictions', *British Journal of Addiction*, 85: pp. 1389–94.

Marlatt, G. A. and George, W. H. (1984) 'Relapse prevention: introduction and overview of the model', *British Journal of Addiction*, 79: pp. 261–73.

Miller, W. (1983) 'Motivational interviewing with problem drinkers', *Behavioural Psychotherapy*, 11: pp. 147–72.

Mitcheson, M., Edwards, G., Hawks, D. and Ogbourne, A. (1976) 'Treatment of Methylamphetamine users during the 1968 epidemic', in Edwards, G., Russell, M. A. H., Hawks, D. and McCafferty, M. (eds), *Drugs and Drug Dependence* (Farnborough: Saxon House/Lexington).

O'Brien, C. P., Chaddock, B., Woody, G. E. and Greenstein, R. (1974) 'Systematic extinction of addiction-associated rituals using narcotic antagonists', *Psychosomatic Medicine*, 36: p. 458.

O'Brien, C. P., Childress, A. R., Arndt, I. O., McLellan, A. T., Woody, M. D. and Many, I. (1988) 'Pharmacologic and behavioural treatments of cocaine dependence. Controlled studies', *Journal of Clinical Psychiatry*, 49(2)(Suppl.): pp. 17–22.

O'Hare, P. A., Newcombe, R., Mathews, A., Buning, E. C. and Drucker,

E. (eds) (1992) *The Reduction of Drug Related Harm* (London: Routledge).

Phillips, G. T., Gossop, M. R., Edwards, G., Sutherland, G., Taylor, C. and Strang, J. (1987) 'The application of the SODQ to the measurement of the severity of opiate dependence in a British sample', *British Journal of Addiction*, 82: pp. 690–700.

Post, R. M. (1975) 'Cocaine Psychoses: A continuum model', *American Journal of Psychiatry*, 132: pp. 225–31.

Powell, J., Gray, J. A., Bradley, B., Kasvikis, Y., Strang, J., Barratt, L. and Marks, I. (1990) 'The effects of exposure to drug-related cues in detoxified opiate addicts: a theoretical review and some new data', *Addictive Behaviors*, 15: pp. 339–54.

Rosenthal, M. (1990) 'The therapeutic community exploring the boundaries', *British Journal of Addiction*, 84: pp. 141–50.

Rounsaville, B. J., Weissman, M. M. and Kleber, H. D. (1983) 'An evaluation of depression in opiate addicts, *Research in Community and Mental Health*, 3: pp. 257–89.

Rounsaville, B. J., Gawin, F. and Kleber, H. (1985) Interpersonal psychotherapy adapted for ambulatory cocaine users, *American Journal of Drug and Alcohol Abuse*, 11(3&4): pp. 171–91.

Spitz, H. I. and Rosencan, J. S. (1987) *Cocaine Abuse: New directions in treatment and research* (New York: Brunner/Mazel).

Stanton, M. D. (1979) 'Family treatment approaches to drug abuse problems: a review', *Family Processes*, 18: pp. 251–75.

Stimson, G. V., Aldritt, L., Dolan, K. and Donoghoe, M. (1988) 'Syringe exchange schemes for drug users in England and Scotland', *British Medical Journal*, 296: p. 1717.

Stimson, G. V., Donoghoe, M. C., Lart, R. and Dolan, K. (1990) 'Distributing sterile needles and syringes to people who inject drugs: the syringe exchange experiment', in Strang, J. and Stimson, G. V. (eds), *AIDS and Drug Misuse: the challenge for policy and practice in the 1990s* (London: Routledge).

Stimson, G. V., 'Harm minimisation', in Strang, J. and Gossop, M. (eds), *Responding to Drug Misuse: the 'British System'* (Oxford: Oxford University Press (in press)).

Stockwell, T. R., Hodgson, R. J., Edwards, G., Taylor, C. and Rankin, H. (1979) 'The development of a questionnaire to measure severity of alcohol dependence', *British Journal of Addiction*, 74: pp. 79–87.

Stockwell, T. (1986) 'What I would still like to know: cracking an old chestnut – is controlled drinking possible for someone who has been severely alcohol dependent?' *British Journal of Addiction*, 81: pp. 455–6.

Strang, J., Griffiths, P. and Gossop, M. (1990) 'Crack and cocaine use in South London drug addicts: 1987–1989', *British Journal of Addiction*, 87: pp. 193–6.

Strang, J. and Farrell, M. (1992) 'Harm minimisation for drug users: when second best may be best first', *British Medical Journal*.

Sutherland, G., Edwards, G., Taylor, C., Phillips, G., Gossop, M. and Brady, R. (1986) 'The measurement of opiate dependence', *British Journal* of Addiction, 81: pp. 485–94.

Tennant, F. S., Jnr and Sagherian, A. A. (1987) 'Double blind comparison of amantadine and bromocryptine for ambulatory withdrawal for cocaine dependence', *Archives of Internal Medicine*, 147: pp. 109–11.

Van Bilsen, H. P. and Van Emst, A. J. (1986) 'Heroin addiction and motivational milieu therapy, *International Journal of the Addictions*, 21: pp. 707–13.

Van Bilsen, H. P. (1988) 'Motivating drug users to change', in Bennett, G. A. (ed.), *New directions in the treatment of drug abuse* (London: Routledge).

Washton, A. M. (1988) 'Preventing relapse to cocaine', *Journal of Clinical Psychiatry*, 49(2 Suppl.): pp. 34–8.

Wells, B., 'Narcotics Anonymous and the self-help movement', in Strang, J. and Gossop, M. (eds), *Responding to Drug Misuse: the 'British System'* (Oxford: Oxford University Press, 1992).

Yates, R. (1985) 'Addiction: an everyday "disease"', in Lishman, J. and Horobin, G. (eds), *Approaches to Addiction* (London: Kogan Page), pp. 91–101.

# Index